POPE
FRANCIS

Family
Devotional

POPE FRANCIS

Family Devotional

---

365 Reflections to Share with Your Kids

Edited by

Rebecca Vitz Cherico

Our Sunday Visitor

www.osv.com
Our Sunday Visitor Publishing Division
Our Sunday Visitor, Inc.
Huntington, Indiana 46750

Quotations from Pope Francis
copyright © by Libreria Editrice Vaticana.

Reflections copyright © 2016 by Rebecca Vitz Cherico.
Published 2016 by Our Sunday Visitor.

21 20 19 18 17 16   1 2 3 4 5 6 7 8 9

Our Sunday Visitor Publishing Division, Our Sunday Visitor, Inc.,
200 Noll Plaza, Huntington, IN 46750; 1-800-348-2440

ISBN: 978-1-68192-014-6 (Inventory No. T1774)
eISBN: 978-1-68192-015-3
LCCN: 2016941234

Cover design: Amanda Falk
Cover art: Giulio Napolitano/Shutterstock.com; Shutterstock
Interior design: Dianne Nelson

PRINTED IN THE UNITED STATES OF AMERICA

Contents

ℭℜ

Introduction

CR

WORKING ON THE REFLECTIONS FOR THIS BOOK has been a real joy: a bit too much work to be pure pleasure, but deeply rewarding and inspiring. I have attempted to get to the heart of what Pope Francis is saying, and how he wants to challenge us, even though his words at times are hard to hear or understand. There were days he spoke about joy that felt far from me, and other times he wrote about suffering I have not known. Like any good teacher, he repeats himself, and I learned to find inspiration in the things he felt most needed repeating. I hope that the repetitions in my own reflections resonate both with his words and your experience.

I kept my own family in mind while writing: both the words my own children would understand and the things that we all need to hear and still need to learn.

Families are different in many ways: when, where, and how you use this book will vary greatly. I hope you feel free to adapt it to your circumstances. I have tried to make it flexible enough to use at different times of the day and for people of different ages and stages of life.

On those days—and I hope they are many!—when you are able to pray with your whole family, you may want to add your own experiences to the reflections and discuss some of the questions with your children—or make up your own.

More than anything, I hope that my reflections allow the truth that Pope Francis communicates to take root. My hope for you is the same one I have for myself: that the words contained here not be dead letters, but that they may bring us all closer to the Lord and to the fullness of his Incarnation.

—Rebecca Cherico, Editor

January 1

Mary Is Always There for Us

Solemnity of Mary, the Holy Mother of God

ⳤ

MARY IS THE MOTHER OF GOD, our mother and mother of the Church. So many men and women, young and old have turned to her to say "thank you" and to beg a favor.

Mary takes us to Jesus and Jesus gives us peace. Let us turn to her, trusting in her assistance, with courage and hope.

~Address, Meeting with Young People,
Castelpetroso, Italy, July 5, 2014

Reflection: Mary is a very loving mother, and she wants to help us more than she cares about being recognized or acknowledged. So we don't need to be embarrassed to ask the same things over and over.

She's happy to help: she has been uniting people to her son from the moment he was conceived.

January 2

Thank You, Lord

ରେ

HOW MANY YOUNG PEOPLE, how many of you, today have the opportunity to study, to sit at the table with your family every day, not to worry about the essentials. How many of you enjoy this? Altogether, those of you who have these things let us say, "Thank you, Lord!"

~Address, Meeting with Young People,
Asunción, Paraguay, July 12, 2015

Reflection: There is a famous joke about two young fish that meet an older fish as they are swimming along. "How's the water?" the older fish asks. After he swishes off, one of the younger fish turns to the other and asks, "What's water?"

So often we take the most basic things for granted—so much that we don't really enjoy or appreciate them. Let us try to see all that we've been given today.

Lord, when I fail to recognize how much I've been given, help me to see it! Lead me to see what I don't!

January 3

Respect for Those in Need

CR

THE POOR PERSON IS JUST LIKE ME and, if he or she is going through a difficult time for many reasons, be they economic, political, social, or personal, it could be me in their place, me longing for someone to help me. As well as desiring this help, if I am in their shoes, I have the right to be respected.

~Address, Meeting with Civic Leaders,
Asunción, Paraguay, July 11, 2015

Reflection: When we think of poor people, we usually think of people without money—and rightly so. But people can be poor in many ways. They can be (or feel) unable to take care of themselves or their families in many ways.

The more I recognize my own poverty—the ways in which I am incapable of taking care of myself or those I love—the more I can look at a person who is poor (financially or otherwise) with compassion and generosity.

Realizing how much I depend on our good and gracious God unites me to my poor neighbor—and brings riches to both our lives.

January 4

Nothing Lukewarm

CR

WE DON'T WANT NAMBY-PAMBIES, young people who are just there, lukewarm, unable to say either yes or no. We don't want young people who tire quickly and who are always weary, with bored faces.

We want young people who are strong. We want young people full of hope and strength. Why? Because they know Jesus, because they know God. Because they have a heart that is free.

~Address, Meeting with Young People,
Asunción, Paraguay, July 12, 2015

Reflection: Parents often complain about strong-willed children—and children don't always like their parents to be strong-willed, either! But being strong-willed isn't just a question of character; it's a question of desire.

Many quiet, unassuming people can be very strong in the face of a real challenge, because the truest desires of their heart are at stake, whereas many people may seem passionate about something until they have to work really hard for it.

But Jesus can sustain us in our enthusiasm and drive, because he answers our deepest desires and allows our passions to come through in all the best ways, whatever temperament God gave us.

January 5

The Precious Gift of Brotherly Love and Sisterly Affection

 C൪

HAVING A BROTHER, A SISTER, who loves you is a deep, precious, irreplaceable experience.

~General Audience, February 18, 2015

Reflection: Having a brother or sister (or many of them) helps us learn to love by giving us people we didn't do anything to get, whether we asked our parents to give us a sibling or not! There is someone else who shares my home, shares my parents, shares so much of my experience—whether our personalities are similar or different.

Having a sibling helps me see clearly that I am not alone in this world or in my experience and helps me understand the depths of God's love—that he gave me what I didn't even know I needed.

January 6

Making Time to Welcome Jesus

❦

EACH CHRISTIAN FAMILY CAN, first of all—as Mary and Joseph did—welcome Jesus, listen to him, speak with him, guard him, protect him, grow with him; and in this way improve the world.

Let us make room in our heart and in our day for the Lord. As Mary and Joseph also did, and it was not easy: how many difficulties they had to overcome! They were not … an unreal family.

~General Audience, December 17, 2015

Reflection: When we look at pictures of the Holy Family, of Mary, Jesus, and Joseph, they look so calm. We can forget all the work and struggles they went through.

Sometimes we have to fight for our time with Jesus, fight to make room in our schedules and in our hearts. But he is worth fighting for.

Jesus, Mary, and Joseph, help me fight to make time for what matters most!

January 7

Signs of Friendship

ભ

ONE OF THE MOST PRECIOUS THINGS about our being Christians is that we are friends, friends of Jesus. When you love someone, you spend time with them, you watch out for them and you help them, you tell them what you are thinking, but also you never abandon them.

That's how Jesus is with us; he never abandons us. Friends stand by one another, they help one another, they protect another. The Lord is like that with us. He is patient with us.

~Address, Meeting with Young People,
Asunción, Paraguay, July 12, 2015

Reflection: Being a good friend is often difficult. Even people you love dearly can disappoint or confuse you. It's tempting to just move on when someone hurts you, to give up or move on, without trying to improve the situation.

Do you know anyone who needs your loyalty and support in a particular way? Is there some way you can be more patient with your friends, just as Jesus is patient with you?

January 8

Caring for Creation with Our Talents

CR

ALL OF US CAN COOPERATE as instruments of God for the care of creation, each according to his or her own … talents.

~Laudato Si', 14

Reflection: Some people love animals, while others aren't really into them. Some people are great at cleaning, while others struggle with it. But whatever particular strengths each of us has, we have all been given the same creation.

We will need to work with others to care for creation, but that is part of God's plan—he wants to see us united in caring for the precious gifts he has given. How can I use my talents to better care for our common gifts?

January 9

Why We Pray

ॐ

Praying always lifts us out of our worries and concerns. It makes us rise above everything that hurts, upsets, or disappoints us, and helps to put ourselves in the place of others, in their shoes.

The family is a school where prayer also reminds us that we are not isolated individuals; we are one and we have a neighbor close at hand: he or she is living under the same roof, is a part of our life, and is in need.

~Homily, Mass for Families,
Guayaquil, Ecuador, July 6, 2015

Reflection: Everything in life is easier if we have someone on our side who loves us. Prayer is so important because it reminds us of that.

Family life isn't easy—just because we live with people doesn't mean we always feel as if they are on our side or that they love us. That's why we need to be patient with our families and ourselves. And we need prayer for that!

January 10

How We Speak Tells Volumes

CR

AT HOME DO WE SHOUT at one another or do we speak with love and tenderness? This is a good way of measuring our love.
~Homily, Closing Mass, World Meeting of Families, Philadelphia, September 27, 2015

Reflection: I don't know about you, but this quote can make me feel guilty: my family is loud. But even if you're a gentler group, you're not off the hook yet: speaking quietly isn't the same as speaking with love and tenderness.

Whatever our family's natural orientation, we are asked to love one another and treat one another accordingly. So we can think: If Jesus were here—would I talk this way? What if this person really *was* Jesus—would I use this tone? We can use our imaginations to understand reality, because he is truly present with us.

January 11

Based on Appearances

CR

[THE DEVIL] IS A CON ARTIST because he tells us that we have to abandon our friends and never to stand by anyone. Everything is based on appearances. He makes you think that your worth depends on how much you possess.

~Address, Meeting with Young People,
Asunción, Paraguay, July 12, 2015

Reflection: Many times, we complain about superficiality and superficial people. But many people, deep down, are afraid that there is nothing more to life. They are superficial because they have bought the devil's lie that life is all about appearances, all about what you have and how you look. It's a terrifying way to live.

We have a chance to show the world how much richer life is when we go beyond appearances, when we stay faithful and true, especially in difficult circumstances. Every time we stay loyal to a friend, we are stealing a piece of the world away from the devil and claiming it for Christ.

January 12

Beginning to Live Again

ᚼ

ANYONE WHO IS DESPERATE AND TIRED TO DEATH, if he entrusts himself to Jesus and to his love, can begin to live again. And to begin a new life, to change life is a way of rising again, of resurrecting.

Faith is a force of life ... and those who believe in Christ must acknowledge this in order to promote life in every situation, in order to let everyone, especially the weakest, experience the love of God who frees and saves.

~Angelus, June 28, 2015

Reflection: I love coffee. I don't need to understand quite how caffeine works in my body to know that coffee helps me wake up in the morning, or how it keeps kids—and some adults—awake at night!

I may not understand quite *how* trusting in Jesus lets me live again, but it does. Where Christ lives, everything resurrects. When I am tired and desperate—or see someone who is—let me remember what makes new life possible.

January 13

Even the Best Need Help

CR

EVEN THE BEST FAMILIES NEED SUPPORT, and it takes a lot of patience to support one another! But such is life. Life is not lived in a laboratory, but in reality. Jesus himself experienced a family upbringing.

~General Audience, May 20, 2015

Reflection: One of my daughters is an excellent cook. Because she is so good, I sometimes give her suggestions on how to improve small things. I do that because I know she'll understand what I tell her and learn from it. What might seem like criticism comes from my great esteem for her.

Family life brings many challenges—and that's okay. It's not a sign that we're messing everything up, it's a sign that we're engaged with a reality that's bigger than we are. Jesus lived in a family himself—he knows that we all have so much to learn from his Father, and that we will need a lot of patience and a lot of courage.

Sometimes we can wish that family life weren't so messy, but life is much better in reality than it is in a laboratory—and messiness is a small price to pay for that difference!

January 14

Starting from Common Ground

CR

WE HAVE TO KNOW HOW TO WELCOME AND ACCEPT those who think differently than we do. Honestly, sometimes we are very closed. We shut ourselves up in our little world: "Either things go my way or not at all."…

If you are different than I am, then why don't we talk? Why do we always throw stones at one another over what separates us, what makes us different? Why don't we extend a hand where we have common ground?

Why not try to speak about what we have in common, and then we can talk about where we differ.

~Address to Students, Havana, Cuba,
September 20, 2015

Reflection: I don't know too many identical twins, but I doubt they sit around talking about how much they have in common: even twins are different!

Sometimes sameness just isn't interesting—but difference doesn't need to divide us. We have the same Father: We're not *that* different. When we remember this, we can always find some common ground to start from, and build from there.

January 15

Patience and Happiness

♋

JESUS KNOWS THAT IN THIS WORLD filled with competition, envy, and aggression, true happiness comes from learning to be patient, from respecting others, from refusing to condemn or judge others.

As the saying goes: "When you get angry, you lose." Don't let your heart give in to anger and resentment.

~Address, Meeting with Young People,
Asunción, Paraguay, July 12, 2015

Reflection: People often worry about winning; their goal is to be successful: winning is fun! But even though we like to win, it's much more satisfying to defeat a really good team or worthy opponent, because we get to test ourselves and *improve* in the process: we get better.

But sometimes we think about winning as something that proves we're better than other people; we get cocky and forget that our own talents were given to us by God.

We can be more talented than others in one way or another, but God loves us all. When we get angry or judge others harshly, we lose God's vision and the opportunity he's offering us to improve. We really do lose, whatever argument or game we've won. Let's remember: When we die, no one is going to ask us for the score.

January 16

Don't Forget to Dream

ॐ

IN ARGENTINA WE SAY: "Don't be a pushover!"... Open up and dream! Dream that with you the world can be different. Dream that if you give your best, you are going to help make this world a different place. Don't forget to dream!

~Address to Students, Havana, Cuba,
September 20, 2015

Reflection: Dr. Martin Luther King Jr.'s most famous speech begins, "I have a dream ..." His dream paved the way for a transformation in American society. Rooted in the certainty that if God had called him to a task, he would find a way, King helped change the world.

When we open up and dream, we open ourselves to discovering our vocations, what it is that we want most, what God has made us for, and where he is leading us.

January 17

The Way, the Truth, and New Life

ℭ℞

LET US LOOK TO JESUS.... He is "the way, and the truth, and the life." He comes to save us from the lie that says no one can change, the lie of thinking that no one can change. Jesus helps us to journey along the paths of life and fulfillment.

May the power of his love and his resurrection always be a path leading you to new life.

~Address, Visit to Detainees, Philadelphia,
September 27, 2015

Reflection: Can people change? Usually we say they can, "but…" We think they *can*, but we don't really believe they *will*.

There are many reasons for our disbelief: We've seen people make New Year's resolutions and give them up the next day; we've seen people swear they'll never touch a drink again, and then they're back at it in a month; we see people pledge to put the cap back on the toothpaste, but then … And what about ourselves? How many times have we seen our own resistance to changing—either because we don't want to change or somehow we can't?

It's not crazy to think that people are unable to change—but it's not Christian. It's not Christian because it is God who brings about real change. We can allow him—they can allow him—but lasting, permanent, real change is possible and comes through him.

When we doubt the ability to change, it's the Lord we doubt. God, give us more faith!

January 18

Seeing the Good

CR

HAPPY ABOVE ALL Are the ones who can see the good in other people.
~Address, Meeting with Young People,
Asunción, Paraguay, July 12, 2015

Reflection: Sometimes it is so easy to be annoyed by people in our family: parents, children, siblings! We can feel like we're being nice—but fake—when we say something good about them. But God wants us to love with wide-open hearts, he wants us to see the good in other people because (a) it's really there, and (b) we will be happier ourselves when we see it.

Lord, please help me to see the good in others today, especially when it's hard for me to find. Let me look for it, knowing it's in there somewhere—and that I will be happier when I can see it more clearly.

January 19

New Kinds of Fishermen

CB

JESUS, WHEN HE CALLED PETER to follow him, told him that he would make him a "fisher of men"; and for this reason a new type of net is needed. We should say that, today, families are one of the most important nets for the mission of Peter and of the Church.

This is not a net that takes one prisoner! On the contrary, it frees people from the cruel waters of abandonment and indifference, which drown many human beings in the sea of loneliness and indifference.

~General Audience, October 7, 2015

Reflection: Sometimes it's hard to see things clearly from the inside. For us families, it often looks like we're just a bunch of fish flopping around, fighting the net.

But if we get a chance to see things from the other side, we recognize that our families are a place where we are brought together, and where others are invited in.

Seeing the love that a family has for each other, the tenderness of affection for its members, even (especially) when they're weak, handicapped, or strange, gives people hope for their own lives. It makes them do what no fish does: to want to happily choose the net.

January 20

He Doesn't Condemn

CR

JESUS KNOWS US BETTER than anyone else; when we sin, he does not condemn us but rather says to us, "Go and sin no more" (Jn 8:11).

~Angelus, September 21, 2014

Reflection: It is said that some of the hardest words to hear are, "I love you, but ..." while some of the nicest words are "... but I love you!" We all make mistakes, but is the last word a word of love or a word of condemnation?

The Lord is merciful: he knows us, and never gets tired of forgiving us. He tells us not to sin, but he loves us even though we do. He tells us daily, "But I love you!"

January 21

Brotherhood Cannot Be Broken

℩

IN THE FAMILY TOO, how many siblings quarrel over little things, or over an inheritance, and then they no longer speak to each other, they no longer greet one another. This is terrible!

Brotherhood is a great thing, when we consider that all our brothers and sisters lived in the womb of the same mother for nine months, came from the mother's flesh! Brotherhood cannot be broken.

~General Audience, February 18, 2015

Reflection: A lot of people fight more with their families than with other people. Many times, that's because we feel more certain of our families—they are our flesh and blood, and so we're not as afraid they will leave us even if they are angry with us.

It's good to be so sure, but sometimes being sure means we take people for granted and treat them badly because we can. And sometimes we let our petty emotions take over and stop being certain of our families—we let money or politics or other things come between us and divide us permanently.

But those things are never as strong as the bond we share. We must never forget that.

January 22

Learning from Jesus, Mary, and Joseph

CR

IT IS CERTAINLY NOT DIFFICULT to imagine how much mothers could learn from Mary's care for [Jesus]! And how much fathers could glean from the example of Joseph, a righteous man, who dedicated his life to supporting and protecting the Child and his wife—his family—in difficult times. Not to mention how much children could be encouraged by the adolescent Jesus to understand the necessity and beauty of cultivating their ... vocation and of dreaming great dreams!

~General Audience, December 17, 2015

Reflection: All of us—parents and children alike—stand to learn from the Holy Family. We don't know much about their life together, and that's probably good because it keeps us from trying to copy them.

What we need to learn from them isn't technical; it's a way of looking at all of life and at each other. With greater trust, affection, and faith, and a greater willingness to sacrifice, knowing that what lies ahead is better than anything we leave behind.

January 23

The Real Way to Influence People

℘

THE LORD SAYS TO US QUITE CLEARLY ... you do not convince people with arguments, strategies, or tactics. You convince them by simply learning how to welcome them.

~Homily, Mass, Asunción, Paraguay,
July 12, 2015

Reflection: Telemarketers and other people who do business on the phone are usually told to smile when they're on a call. The person on the other end cannot see the smile, but they can hear it in their voice—it changes the way a person sounds.

In the Gospel, we see how often people's encounters with Jesus changed their lives. We know what he said and did, but we have to imagine how he said and did it. But if we've met him in prayer, for example, or in the sacraments, and have been changed by him, we can imagine it. We understand how his look penetrated them, how he loved them and welcomed and forgave them all at once. We've all been looked at like that.

Let us pray: Jesus, let us remember your merciful gaze on us when it is our turn to welcome others.

January 24
Don't Be Afraid to Give Your Best

જી

RESIST THE GROWING MENTALITY which considers it useless and absurd to aspire to things that demand effort. "There's no point getting involved, it can no longer be fixed." This attitude belittles those who ... want to move forward. Be committed to something; be committed to someone....

Don't be afraid to take a risk on the field, but play fairly and give it your best. Don't be afraid to give the best of yourselves! Don't look for easy solutions beforehand so as to avoid tiredness and struggle. And don't bribe the referee.

~Address, Meeting with Civic Leaders,
Asunción, Paraguay, July 11, 2015

Reflection: Sometimes we don't want to do our best because we are afraid: afraid of looking stupid if we don't manage to succeed in what we try to do. We don't realize that the risk of *not* trying is much bigger: we risk going through life without ever really getting interested in things, bored most of the time. Deep down, we're bored with ourselves.

But living that way, we never understand who we are or what we most desire. Trying our best—even when we fail—is the only way to be ourselves.

Jesus can free us from the fear of failure; he gives us the freedom to be our whole selves and the hope to try even when the outcome is uncertain.

January 25

The Treasure of the Elderly

CR

WHILE WE ARE YOUNG, we are led to ignore old age, as if it were a disease to keep away from; then when we become old, especially if we are poor, if we are sick and alone, we experience the shortcomings of a society ... which ... ignores its elderly. And the elderly are a wealth not to be ignored.

~General Audience, March 4, 2015

Reflection: People often become more religious if they are diagnosed with a fatal illness. Being close to death makes them think about their lives in a new and more meaningful way. The elderly—knowing they are closer to death than when they were young—are more inclined to think about life in a truer way: their lives and perspective are richer in understanding than younger people's.

We rob ourselves when we don't see their wisdom and avoid them instead of seeking them out.

January 26

Not Afraid of Questions

CR

JESUS IS NOT AFRAID of people's questions; he is not afraid of our humanity or the different things we are looking for. On the contrary, he knows the depths of the human heart, and, as a good teacher, he is always ready to encourage and support us.

~Homily, Mass, Havana, Cuba,
September 20, 2015

Reflection: When we are certain that something is true, we're not afraid of someone's questions about it, even if we do not have all the answers. But we get nervous when we're afraid they will catch us in a lie, or when we have to admit we don't know or understand something.

Let's not let our pride confuse us! There may be things we don't know, but nothing that is really true is contrary to the truth of Christianity. It may be difficult to understand—some things are beyond our understanding—but there is no genuine truth that contradicts the reality of Christ. So we don't need to be afraid to accompany our friends and family as they try to understand their—and our—lives and faith better.

January 27

Beginning Again

CR

AT TIMES, STORMS FROM WITHOUT AND WITHIN force us to tear down what had been built and to begin again, but always with the hope given us by God.

~Address, Vespers, Asunción,
Paraguay, July 11, 2015

Reflection: Looking for a job can sometimes feel like a full-time job itself. Perhaps that is why many people don't start looking seriously for a new job until they lose the one they had.

It can be hard to start fresh or build something new when old structures are still in place—and sometimes even harder when loss comes upon us suddenly and we feel the anxiety of what we'll do if we don't find a way to build a new house or get a new job.

But whatever our circumstances, we are all called to start again. God can take away our fear of loss; he reminds us that he is with us always. Whatever storms blow through our lives, he has not left us and wants to build something beautiful with us—more beautiful than whatever we have lost.

Lord, let me never be afraid to begin again, knowing that you are by my side.

January 28

No Need to Show Off

CR

THE LORD ... "DID NOT REGARD EQUALITY WITH GOD as something to be [grasped]" (Phil 2:6).... A person called by God does not show off; he or she does not seek recognition or applause; he or she does not claim to be better than others, standing apart as if on a pedestal.

~ Address, Vespers, Asunción,
Paraguay, July 11, 2015

Reflection: Many times, people who seem like they have the biggest egos turn out to be really insecure and unhappy. Everybody likes to feel appreciated and important, but when we need to feel appreciated and important all the time, something is wrong. When we know we really *are* important, we don't need to show off.

Jesus knew how important he was, because he was totally confident and secure in his relationship with his heavenly Father. He was so sure that even when he was betrayed and put to death, he didn't lose his certainty (even though he was scared and sad).

Do I know how precious I am in God's eyes? Do I have any idea how much he loves me?

January 29

God Gives Us Himself

ℭ

MAY GOD OUR FATHER look upon our hearts; may God our Father who loves us give us his strength, his patience, his fatherly tenderness, and may he bless us.

~Address, Rehabilitation Center,
Santa Cruz de la Sierra, Bolivia,
July 10, 2015

Reflection: God wants to give us good things, but most of all he wants to give us the most precious gift he has: himself. Let's pray to have his tenderness, that the blessing we seek most from him be himself, to look at the world with his same mercy and compassion.

January 30

Called to Mercy

છ

THE MERCY TO WHICH WE ARE CALLED embraces all of creation, which God entrusted to us so that we keep it, not exploit it or, worse still, destroy it. We must always seek to leave the world better than we found it (cf. Encyclical *Laudato Si'*, 194), beginning with the environment in which we live and the small gestures of our daily life.

~General Audience, October 28, 2015

Reflection: The Boy Scouts have long had a pledge to leave a place better than they found it. This small thing is part of the great appeal the Scouts have had to many over the years. Picking trash up off the ground, flushing toilets in public restrooms, not using all the hot water for our own shower: these are gestures of love and respect both to the natural environment and the people we live with.

Helping care for common spaces communicates a concern that surpasses cultural and personal differences.

January 31

Come Back!

CR

NONE OF US KNOWS what life will bring us. And you, dear young friends, are asking, "What is in store for me?" We are capable of doing bad things, very bad things, but please, do not despair: the Father is always there waiting for us!

Come back! Come back! This is the word: Come back!

Come back home because the Father is waiting for me. And if I am a great sinner, he will celebrate the more.

~Address, Meeting with Asian Youth,
Dangjin, South Korea, August 15, 2014

Reflection: Our world today is not very comfortable with the word sin. We don't like thinking of ourselves as committing sin; it seems like that's calling people bad—including ourselves. In a way, that's true.

But recognizing that we are *all* sinful is also freeing: we can see that it's not our sin that defines us; God doesn't love us because we're perfect or because he thinks we are. He knows better than that! But he wants us, and he loves us right now. What are we waiting for?

February 1

We Can Always Make Amends

CR

EVEN IF YOU MAKE MISTAKES, make amends, get up again and move forward—make progress with concrete steps.

~Address, Meeting with Civic Leaders,
Asunción, Paraguay, July 11, 2015

Reflection: Most people feel very embarrassed if they fall in a public place. They want to act like nothing happened, but are afraid everyone has already noticed and is laughing at them—so they usually want to get up fast. Sometimes we could use a little of that fire when we fall in other parts of our life!

Of course, we make mistakes—even Jesus wasn't able to carry his cross the whole way alone. But he got up again, and so can we—with his assistance.

February 2

Commitment and Sacrifice

CR

WORDS ON THEIR OWN ARE NOT ENOUGH. If you give your word of honor, then make sacrifices each day to be faithful to that word, to be committed!

~Address, Meeting with Civic Leaders,
Asunción, Paraguay, July 11, 2015

Reflection: Words are powerful, and sometimes it is hard to live up to our promises. But the more we stick with it and do what we've promised—in our families, with our friends, at school, to God—the more we learn to be faithful in word and deed.

Lord, help me to keep my promises! Do not let me cheapen my word or myself by saying I'll do things I won't.

February 3

Strength in Knowing Jesus

CR

TO KNOW GOD IS STRENGTH. In other words, to know God, to draw closer to Jesus, is hope and strength. And that is what we need from young people today: young people full of hope and strength.

~Address, Meeting with Young People,
Asunción, Paraguay, July 12, 2015

Reflection: God is the source of our strength: he's the one who makes us strong. This means that we can be hopeful in every moment and every situation in life, no matter how bad things are.

Lord, give us your hope today. Show us how we can be strong in you even when we feel tired or weak. Remind us that when we look for strength in you, instead of in ourselves, our hope springs eternal.

February 4

We Don't Fight Alone

CR

I ASK YOU NOT TO FIGHT THE GOOD FIGHT ALONE. Try to talk about these things among yourselves, profit from the lives, the stories of your elders, of your grandparents, for there is great wisdom there. "Waste" lots of time listening to all the good things they have to teach you.

~Address, Meeting with Civic Leaders,
Asunción, Paraguay, July 11, 2015

Reflection: Once I visited my grandmother with several friends. I had spent a lot of time with her before, but there were many things we never talked about. My friends asked her questions I never had, and she told stories I'd never heard before: amazing stories, full of wisdom and humor.

Wise and wonderful people surround us, but we need to talk to them! Sometimes those conversations take time we don't think we have.

Are we sure all the things we are so busy doing are more important? Can I take the time to talk to an older person—not just to be nice, but rather because I might really learn something?

February 5

Keep Smiling

༄

KEEP SMILING AND HELP BRING JOY to everyone you meet. It isn't
always easy.

~Address, Meeting with Immigrant Families,
Harlem, New York City, September 25, 2015

Reflection: We always appreciate it when someone gives us a
genuine smile. But, as the pope says, it's not always easy to do: it's
hard to bring joy when you don't have it! It's good to know, though,
that the very act of smiling actually activates a response in our brain
that makes us happier: smiling at someone else changes us, too.

But even when we don't feel joyful or happy, or willing to
smile, we can always pray. God knows how to use us to bring his
joy to others, even if we're not feeling as glad as we'd like. Knowing
that God is using us for his greater glory can bring us gladness in
spite of ourselves.

February 6

Jesus Is Very Near to His Children

☙

LET US NEVER FORGET that Jesus is close to his children. He is very near, in our hearts. Never hesitate to pray to him, to talk to him, to share with him your questions and your pain. He is always with us, he is ever near, and he will not let us fall.

~Address to Sick Children, Pediatric Hospital,
Asunción, Paraguay, July11, 2015

Reflection: In the Book of Deuteronomy, we learn that God's law is inscribed in our hearts. Sometimes God comes to us through people we can see and touch and who may visit us when we're sick. But even when those people are far away, we have him inscribed in our hearts. We can always speak to him in prayer. And he is always there, already waiting for us.

February 7

Peace Between Brothers

❧

LET THERE BE AN END TO WARS BETWEEN BROTHERS! Let us always build peace! A peace which grows stronger day by day, a peace which makes itself felt in everyday life, a peace to which each person contributes by seeking to avoid signs of arrogance, hurtful words … and instead by working to foster understanding … and cooperation.

~Address, Meeting with Government Leaders, Paraguay, July 13, 2015

Reflection: When we get into fights, the natural direction is toward escalation. My brother hits me, so I hit him back—*harder.* My sister takes my favorite Halloween candy, so I take her *whole bag.*

The original law of "an eye for an eye and a tooth for a tooth" was actually a way of trying to deal with this—telling people that you could take (only one!) eye from someone who'd taken yours, and (only one!) tooth from someone who removed yours.

We have to work hard to take things in the other direction, to scale down and be merciful. But isn't it better to live in a world where people can still see with both their eyes and smile with all of their teeth?

February 8

Strength Despite the Pain

ෆ

PAIN DOES NOT STIFLE THE HOPE deep within the human heart ...
life goes on, finding new strength even in the midst of difficulties.
~Address, Rehabilitation Center, Santa Cruz
de la Sierra, Bolivia, July 10, 2015

Reflection: Sometimes we think the biggest difficulty we have
in life is avoiding pain and problems. We want to rid ourselves of
difficulties so we can get back to the business of living. But pain
and struggle are a part of life, and even part of what makes life interesting—they become obstacles only when we don't have hope in
something greater than our difficulties.

Let's set our sights on what helps us in our trial, on the One
who made us with hearts that keep hoping even when life is hard.

February 9

What I Have to Offer

CR

[I AM] A MAN WHO HAS EXPERIENCED FORGIVENESS. A man who was, and is, saved from his many sins. That is who I am.

I don't have much more to give you or to offer you, but I want to share with you what I do have and what I love. It is Jesus Christ, the mercy of the Father.

~Address, Rehabilitation Center, Santa Cruz
de la Sierra, Bolivia, July 10, 2015

Reflection: Sometimes we get in trouble for things we didn't do—this usually makes us upset and angry. But do we realize how often we don't get in trouble for things we *have* done?

When it comes to God, do I realize how much I have been forgiven? How many things I've done wrong, but especially how little I even realize or appreciate how much God has done for me? And how much he still wants to do for me? This is all the pope has to offer us. He says it's not much—but it's everything.

February 10

Prayer Is Never Lost

CR

PETER AND PAUL, DISCIPLES OF JESUS, were also prisoners. They …
lost their freedom. But there was something that … did not let
them sink into darkness and meaninglessness. That something was
prayer; it was prayer. Prayer, both individually and with others. They
prayed, and they prayed for one another.

~Address, Rehabilitation Center, Santa Cruz
de la Sierra, Bolivia, July 10, 2015

Reflection: One of the best things about prayer is that it's always
possible. I might not be able to do much, but I can always pray—
wherever I am, however I feel.

God is always with me, and while he doesn't always answer my
prayers the way I would like, he is always listening and coming to
me in prayer. Let me remember to pray always, and never lose hope.

February 11

In the Wounds of Jesus

⋈

IF THERE ARE TIMES WHEN WE EXPERIENCE SADNESS, when we're in a bad way, when we're depressed or have negative feelings, I ask you to look at Christ crucified. Look at his face. He sees us; in his eyes there is a place for us.

We can all bring to Christ our wounds, our pain, our mistakes, our sins, and all those things which perhaps we got wrong. In the wounds of Jesus, there is a place for our own wounds.

~Address, Rehabilitation Center, Santa Cruz
de la Sierra, Bolivia, July 10, 2015

Reflection: When something bad happens to someone, we often try to give advice. This can be helpful, but often what people need most is someone to stay with them.

We need to know that we are not alone in our suffering, that there is someone who is willing to mourn with us, not just tell us what we should do differently or how we can feel better. Jesus understands.

Lord, when bad things happen and I feel like no one understands, show me your presence; remind me that you are with me always.

February 12
Our Precious Religious Freedom

CR

AMERICAN CATHOLICS ARE COMMITTED to building a society which is truly tolerant and inclusive, to safeguarding the rights of individuals and communities, and to rejecting every form of unjust discrimination. With countless other people of good will, they are likewise concerned that efforts to build a just and wisely ordered society respect their deepest concerns and their right to religious liberty.

That freedom remains one of America's most precious possessions.... All are called to be vigilant, precisely as good citizens, to preserve and defend that freedom from everything that would threaten or compromise it.

~Address, Welcoming Ceremony,
Washington, D.C., September 23, 2015

Reflection: One of the great gifts of Christianity to the world is the way that Christ's sacrifice opened the door to the unity and dignity of all people. Christ did not come for just one group of people: he came to save all of us, which is why Christianity is a missionary religion.

Christ helps us recognize the precious value and dignity of every person, at every stage of life. The call to protect religious freedom is a reminder that the light of Christ is a gift for all peoples, not just those who call themselves Christian.

February 13

Don't Be Afraid to Help

☞

HELP ONE ANOTHER. Do not be afraid to help one another. The devil wants quarrels, rivalry, division, gangs. Don't let him play with you. Keep working to make progress, together.

~Address, Rehabilitation Center, Santa Cruz de la Sierra, Bolivia, July 10, 2015

Reflection: Lots of companies do "team building" exercises in which people have to work together. When I work with someone else on a team, I often come to appreciate him or her more—even though I know the other person isn't perfect. I'm not either! But together we can do more than either of us can alone.

Even if someone isn't the best player, we get more done for our team if we stick together than if we stay on the sidelines or, worse, decide to play on opposite sides.

February 14

Hearts Are Made to Be Touched

☙

A HEART USED TO PASSING BY without letting itself be touched; a life which passes from one thing to the next, without ever sinking roots in the lives of the people around us....We could call this "the spirituality of zapping." It is always on the move, but it has nothing to show for it.

There are people who keep up with the latest news, the most recent bestsellers, but ... never manage to connect with others, to strike up a relationship, to get involved, even with the Lord whom they follow.

~Address, Meeting with Clergy, Santa Cruz
de la Sierra, Bolivia, July 9, 2015

Reflection: We have restless hearts. As long as we fight that truth we continue to be restless in so many other ways as well.

We know, deep down, that nothing simply of this world will satisfy us, and so it's easy to flit from one thing to the next without ever really tasting or testing it in its fullness—that way we don't taste the full bitterness of disappointment.

We can say we're busy or not that interested, but deep down we're scared, scared that what we long for can never come true. When we discover the Lord's fullness, we don't need to be afraid of staying with others, putting down roots, taking our time with things, because we start to realize that *in him* we find our fullness.

Nothing else will ever be enough—only God. Let us have the courage today to test and see if he is enough. We don't need to be afraid, because he is.

February 15

The Word That Kills Loneliness

ભ

[JESUS] IS A WORD which breaks the silence of loneliness.
~Homily, Mass, Asunción, Paraguay, July 12, 2015

Reflection: When I was child, I was very scared of the dark, especially when I was out in the country. I tried talking myself out of my fear, but it didn't work. I was okay if I had someone with me, but if I woke up in the middle of the night and had to use the bathroom, I was on my own.

The only thing that calmed me down was to say Jesus' name over and over. Nothing else worked. He walked with me on those dark nights. He alone kept me from being afraid and alone. Jesus, come!

February 16

Family: A Reminder That Life is Worth Living!

ભ

THE PRESENCE AND SUPPORT OF FAMILIES are so important! Grand-parents, fathers, mothers, brothers, sisters, couples, children: all of them remind us that life is worth living and that we should keep fighting for a better world.

~Address, Rehabilitation Center, Santa Cruz
de la Sierra, Bolivia, July 10, 2015

Reflection: When we are children, we can't wait to grow up. When we grow up, we wish we were kids again. We always long for more in life, and seeing the different ways that life is lived by the young and old gives us a sense of perspective; it helps us understand that life can be rich and beautiful under all sorts of different circumstances.

February 17

God Likes Bridges Better than Our Walls

◌ঽ

GOD ALWAYS DESIRES TO BUILD BRIDGES; we are the ones who build walls! And those walls always fall down!

~General Audience, October 14, 2015

Reflection: God always wants to be with us. We are the ones who refuse him. The joke is on us. Where can we go that he cannot find us? Why do we try to block him out?

Most important, why do we stay put, spinning our wheels, when God has provided us with a bridge to heaven?

February 18

Suffering Is a School

CR

THE WEAKNESS AND SUFFERING of our dearest and most cherished loved ones can be, for our children and grandchildren, a school of life—it's important to teach the children, the grandchildren to understand this closeness in illness at home—and they become so when times of illness are accompanied by prayer and the affectionate and thoughtful closeness of relatives.

The Christian community really knows that the family, in the trial of illness, should not be left on its own.

~General Audience, June 10, 2015

Reflection: Sickness in a family is painful for everyone, not just for the sick person, but it is also an opportunity for everyone. That's why sickness and suffering can be a beautiful school. Caring for the sick helps everyone learn that they are loved and cared for even when they feel like a burden.

There is no circumstance or situation where we are left alone. It is best when this unity is reflected both within the family and within the Church—just as no person is left alone, no family should be left alone to fend for themselves, either. We can bring meals to each other, watch each other's children, or just be there to listen. In this way, one person's cross lifts everyone around him.

February 19

A Chosen People

CR

FREQUENTLY WE LACK THE STRENGTH to keep hope alive. How often have we experienced situations which dull our memory, weaken our hope, and make us lose our reason for rejoicing! And then a kind of sadness takes over.

We think only of ourselves, we forget that we are a people … loved, a chosen people.

~Homily, Mass, Santa Cruz de la Sierra,
Bolivia, July 9, 2015

Reflection: Lots of people who are bullied become bullies themselves; lots of people who were treated badly when they were kids treat others badly when they grow up—it becomes an ugly and vicious cycle.

The biggest challenge of hardship is whether we let it harden our hearts. Even if we don't say it out loud, we think that we have a right to treat people the way they've treated us.

But we forget about Our Lord, how much he has loved us, how much he has given us. Let's not ever forget that fact; it is what breaks the vicious cycle and lets us live in love, even when things get hard.

February 20

Jesus Cares for Our Dignity

☙

[JESUS] IS CONCERNED WITH PEOPLE.... Jesus never detracts from the dignity of anyone, no matter how little they possess or seem capable of contributing. He takes everything as it comes.

~Homily, Mass, Santa Cruz de la Sierra,
Bolivia, July 9, 2015

Reflection: It can be difficult to understand the way God sees and judges things. It helps to remember that his ways are not our ways: we tend to be interested in people because they're powerful or good-looking or rich or smart. Those aren't bad things, but they're not what he's after.

Being open-minded means being open to the surprising ways that he reveals himself in unexpected people and places. And wouldn't I rather be happily surprised?

February 21

God Multiplies

൦ൠ

LIFE IS ALWAYS A GIFT which, when placed in the hands of God, starts to multiply. Our Father never abandons us; he makes everything multiply.

~Homily, Mass, Santa Cruz de la Sierra,
Bolivia, July 9, 2015

Reflection: In the biblical story of Noah and the flood, it seems as if God had given up on his creation and just wanted to wipe out what he had made. But when God asked Noah to build the ark, he asked him to bring two of every animal with him. God didn't just want animals to survive as souvenirs, he wanted animals that could reproduce and multiply.

There are times when it seems like things aren't working out or parts of life aren't bearing fruit. In those moments, instead of giving up, we can give things over. When we hand things over to him and trust in his faithfulness to us—without giving up—we start to see unexpected fruit in our life. Things happen.

Lord, grant me the confident courage today to hand things over to you, without giving up on them.

February 22

Love the Poor

☙

LOVE YOUR COUNTRY, your fellow citizens, and, above all, love the poor.

~Address, Meeting with Civic Leaders,
Asunción, Paraguay, July 11, 2015

Reflection: God wants us to love everyone, but we need to start with those closest to us. They are often both the easiest *and* the hardest to love! Our own family, our own country, our own people—learning to love the people we know best is the place to start.

And if we take that love seriously, it leads us naturally to the poor, because the better we know people, the better we know their needs. Let's not be afraid to love people to the point of feeling their needs.

February 23

Don't Be Lazy!

☙

DO NOT LIE, do not steal, and do not be lazy.

~Address, Meeting with Civic Leaders,
La Paz, Bolivia, July 8, 2015

Reflection: We shouldn't lie, and we shouldn't steal: most of us know this. Usually, we realize we're not supposed to do bad things (even if we sometimes do them anyway). But it's a lot easier to fool ourselves into thinking that being lazy or not doing something isn't so bad.

It doesn't seem like a big deal to accidentally keep something that we borrowed from someone else, or "forget" to do something, or ignore a friend.

God wants us to say "no" to bad things, but more than anything he wants us to say "yes" to him. That is what matters most of all: God doesn't want us on the sidelines, he wants us in the game, with our whole selves.

February 24

Brothers and Sisters in Every Person

☙

WE CANNOT BELIEVE IN GOD THE FATHER without seeing a brother or sister in every person, and we cannot follow Jesus without giving our lives for those for whom he died on the cross.

~Address, Welcome Ceremony,
La Paz, Bolivia, July 8, 2015

Reflection: When your mother has a new child—a new brother or a sister—you never know who you'll get. We'd like to choose our family members, but we don't get to! We are called to love people we didn't choose and sometimes don't even like. This can make family life difficult sometimes, but it is a great help in teaching us to love and sacrifice.

We can follow Christ on the cross by trying to love people we didn't choose—our own family members and our brothers and sisters in Christ.

February 25

Christ's Underdogs

CR

PERSEVERANCE IN MISSION is not about going from house to house, looking for a place where we will be more comfortably welcomed. It means casting our lot with Jesus to the end....

To persevere [in telling people about Jesus] even though we are rejected, despite the darkness and growing uncertainty and dangers—this is what we are called to do, in the knowledge that we are not alone, that God's Holy People walk with us.

~Address, Meeting with Clergy, Religious
and Seminarians, Quito, Ecuador, July 8, 2015

Reflection: Most of us like stories and movies about underdogs, people who didn't look like they could succeed. But they did: they succeeded anyway! We root for them because we know, somehow, that they have what it takes—they can make it, if someone will just give them a chance.

Persevering in mission is being an underdog for Christ. If he has called us, and cast us in a starring role, we will come out on top!

February 26

Recovering the Common Good

CR

HOW DO WE HELP OUR YOUNG PEOPLE not to see a university degree as synonymous with higher status, with more money or social prestige? It is not synonymous with that. How can we help make their education a mark of greater responsibility in the face of today's problems, the needs of the poor, concern for the environment?

~Address, Meeting with Educators,
Quito, Ecuador, July 7, 2015

Reflection: In many American families, it's a great moment of achievement when the first person in the family graduates from college: it's a sign of success for everyone. The experience of going to college isn't just for the student; it means greater opportunity for all involved.

Just as the family sacrifices to send their children to college, the kids know that they also have a responsibility to use their education for everyone's benefit. Can we embrace this attitude of social responsibility in our own family and help society to recover this perspective?

February 27

Still a Family, Despite Our Fights

☙

IN FAMILIES, EVERYONE CONTRIBUTES to the common purpose, everyone works for the common good, not denying each person's individuality but encouraging and supporting it. They quarrel, but there is something that does not change: the family bond. Family disputes are resolved afterward.

The joys and sorrows of each are felt by all. That is what it means to be a family!

~Address, Meeting with Civic Leaders,
Quito, Ecuador, July 7, 2015

Reflection: Sometimes the fights in a family can get really ugly! It isn't surprising, really—we can be so different! What is more important than whether we fight is whether we make up—and whether we try to enjoy each other and have fun together or just ignore each other when we're done fighting.

February 28

Language of Love

ରେ

LOVE IS EXPRESSED more by actions than by words.... In every person, in concrete situations, in our life together.... Love is always communicated, it always leads to communication, never to isolation.

~Address, Meeting with Civic Leaders,
Quito, Ecuador, July 7, 2015

Reflection: There are many people who aren't really interested in learning a foreign language, but who decide to learn because they fall in love with someone who speaks that language.

Love always looks for a way to communicate, by saying or doing or giving something. And it doesn't matter if I don't feel like it: If I learn to communicate love, I can express it even when it's hard and I don't think I want to.

Lord, show me how I can better communicate my love.

February 29

The Upside of Sibling Rivalry

ॐ

PARENTS KNOW THAT ALL THEIR CHILDREN are equally loved, even though each has his or her own character. But ... when [the mother] is pregnant [sometimes] a child in the family starts behaving strangely, starts moving away, because he or she sees a clear red traffic light saying "beware because there is now competition," "beware because you are now no longer the only child."

It makes you think. The love of their parents helps children to overcome their selfishness, to learn to live with the newcomer and with others, to yield and be patient.

~Address, Meeting with Civic Leaders,
Quito, Ecuador, July 7, 2015

Reflection: It's easier to be generous when we realize how much we've been given; it's easier to love when we know how much we've been loved. Most children who know that their parents love them are excited when a new sibling arrives.

But when the older children start focusing on themselves, and comparing "what they get" to "what the baby gets," they become upset—even though they may love the baby! But when they realize that the baby needs love, too, they learn to get past their selfishness.

Many times in life, we can choose between focusing either on what someone else gets or on how much love we've already received.

Let's make life easier for everybody by focusing on who loves me—and by helping others do the same by showing them our love!

March 1

Success That Looks Like Failure

ᑫ

THE CROSS SHOWS US A DIFFERENT WAY of measuring success. Ours is to plant the seeds: God sees to the fruits of our labors. And if at times our efforts and works seem to fail and produce no fruit, we need to remember that we are followers of Jesus … and his life, humanly speaking, ended in failure, in the failure of the cross.

~Homily, Vespers, New York City,
September 25, 2015

Reflection: Did you ever think what a failure Jesus might look like on paper, if we use our way of judging things? After thirty years of living at home, he began his public life. After three years, he had a dozen or so faithful followers, most of whom deserted him—one of the guys he trusted most gave him up to the other side—and he was put to death naked, as a petty criminal.

Sure, it was a different era, but he never got any special degrees, wrote anything important, or built any significant buildings. He never got married and never made any money.

I can hardly write these words, because it's so obvious how wrong my standard is. We would judge *God*—God himself—to be a failure?! And who are we to judge? What do we do that we think is so impressive? We need to rethink the way we understand the value of our time and of our lives.

It is our job to say "yes," but God gives the success—and he measures it very differently, and with infinitely greater love, than we do.

March 2

Starting with the Basic Questions

CR

BEGIN LENT WITH SMALL QUESTIONS that will help one to consider: "What is my life like?"... "Who is God for me? Do I choose the Lord? How is my relationship with Jesus?"

[And then ask]: "How is your relationship with your family: with your parents; with your siblings; with your wife; with your husband; with your children?"... We will surely find things that we need to correct.

~Homily, *Domus Sanctae Marthae*,
February 19, 2015

Reflection: Teachers like to say that there is no such thing as a dumb question. The fact is, some of the most basic, the "dumbest," questions are the ones we need to ask the most.

Sometimes, we don't like to ask them, because we don't want to hear the answers! But that's okay! Let's have the courage to ask dumb, hard questions today, knowing the Lord will help answer them in our lives.

March 3
What Are You Going to Do?

CR

WHEN [ST. KATHARINE DREXEL] SPOKE TO POPE LEO XIII of the needs of the missions, the Pope … asked her pointedly: "What about you? What are you going to do?"

Those words changed Katharine's life….Those words—"What about you?"—were addressed to a young person, a young woman with high ideals, and they changed her life. They made her think of the immense work that had to be done, and to realize that she was being called to do her part.

~Homily, Mass, Philadelphia,
September 26, 2015

Reflection: I was once in a class with a professor known to be a great Dante scholar. A student asked him a particular question about the *Divine Comedy*, and he answered: "That's a great question. You should write a paper on it!"

Sometimes, we go to an authority—or to God himself—with concerns or questions, expecting him to take care of things. But those concerns may be a sign of his call to me, personally. I am being asked to learn, to change, to give *my*self. This probably isn't quite what we were expecting—but it's a great thing!

March 4

True Revolution

ભ

WHEN WE GIVE OF OURSELVES, we discover our true identity as children of God in the image of the Father and, like him, givers of life; we discover that we are brothers and sisters of Jesus.... This is the new revolution—for our faith is always revolutionary—this is our deepest and most enduring cry.

~Homily, Mass, Quito, Ecuador,
July 7, 2015

Reflection: People say it's better to give than to receive. But do we really believe it? As long as we think life is about things, of course it's not true! But when we start giving, really giving, we find that life changes; we start to discover a whole new world. The discovery of that world makes a revolution possible, in our hearts and in our lives.

March 5

Looking Even When It Hurts

ભ

ONE THING IS CERTAIN: We can no longer turn our backs on reality, on our brothers and sisters, on mother earth. It is wrong to turn aside from what is happening all around us, as if certain situations did not exist or have nothing to do with our life. It is not right for us, nor is it even humane to get caught up in the play of a throw-away culture.

~Address, Meeting with Educators,
Quito, Ecuador, July 7, 2015

Reflection: It's uncomfortable looking at ugly or sad things. We have a lot of ways of blocking out things we don't want to see or hear: headphones, plugging our ears, looking at mobile devices, or just turning away. Many people don't want to watch the news or read the newspaper because of all the terrible things they have to hear about.

It's true that many times we focus on the bad—but ignoring the hurt and pain in the world doesn't make them go away. Learning to look at the truth—even when it hurts—is necessary to living as Christians.

Lord, help me not to look away from painful realities. Give me your strength to love the truth more than my comfort.

March 6

The Victory of the Cross

CR

WITH [JESUS], EVIL, SUFFERING, AND DEATH do not have the last word, because he gives us hope and life: He has transformed the Cross from being an instrument of hate, defeat, and death to being a sign of love, victory, triumph, and life.

~Address, Way of the Cross,
Rio de Janeiro, Brazil, July 26, 2013

Reflection: Traditionally, theater has been divided into categories called genres. One of the most important has been tragedy. A tragic story is often beautiful, but it ends badly.

In Christianity, tragedy is no longer possible: what looked like the greatest tragedy in the world—God himself being put to death—ended in victory. What can we be truly afraid of?

March 7

What's It All for?

☙

WE HAVE RECEIVED THIS EARTH as an inheritance, as a gift, in trust. We would do well to ask ourselves: "What kind of world do we want to leave behind? What meaning or direction do we want to give to our lives? Why have we been put here? What is the purpose of our work and all our efforts?" (cf. *Laudato Si'*, 160). Why are we studying?

~Address, Meeting with Educators,
Quito, Ecuador, July 7, 2015

Reflection: Sometimes the smartest road to take is a U-turn; and sometimes we just need to stop and look at the map. This is true when we're driving, but also in life. People can get caught up in the rat race of extremely competitive, intense activity. Even people who aren't competitive can feel as if they're on a treadmill: always the same—but never getting to stop.

It helps to ask ourselves—and ask the Lord in prayer—what it is that we really want. What is all our activity for? Is it time to take a break—or even to turn around?

March 8

Led by the Spirit

☙

THE SPIRIT DOES NOT ABANDON US. He becomes one with us so that we can encounter paths of new life. May he, the Spirit, always be our companion and our teacher along the way.

~Address, Meeting with Educators,
Quito, Ecuador, July 7, 2015

Reflection: Many bad things and hardships may come our way: Jesus warned us about that. But he also promised us that the Spirit will *never* abandon us. Do we look for the Spirit with that confidence?

March 9

Learning from the Saints

ॐ

THE SAINTS CALL US to imitate them and to learn from them.
~Address, Quito, Ecuador, July 6, 2015

Reflection: You can't argue with success, they say. Most saints weren't successful in the worldly sense. But they grew close to God: close enough to be with him in heaven now. That is true success. How can we learn from the saints? What can the saints teach me now about what being successful really means?

March 10

Meaning in Suffering

ଔ

CHRISTIANS KNOW THAT SUFFERING cannot be eliminated, yet it can have meaning and become an act of love and entrustment into the hands of God who does not abandon us; in this way it can serve as a moment of growth in faith and love.

~*Lumen Fidei*, June 29, 2013

Reflection: We live in a scary world, and we worry. We worry about what bad things might happen to us and the people we love, and what good things might not happen.

Christ's suffering was and is a mysterious thing: why should God come to earth to die? But it also freed us from the worst part of suffering: thinking it's meaningless, thinking nothing good can come out of it, thinking we are alone when we suffer.

When we come to understand these things, suffering doesn't go away, but we can live through our pain with the certain hope that it will bring us greater faith and love.

March 11

Stopping the Spread of Spiritual Deserts

ભ

SO MANY OF OUR OWN FRIENDS AND CONTEMPORARIES ... are suffering from spiritual poverty, loneliness, and quiet despair. God seems to be removed from the picture. It is almost as though a spiritual desert is beginning to spread throughout our world....

Yet this is the world into which you are called to go forth and bear witness to the Gospel of hope, the Gospel of Jesus Christ, and the promise of his kingdom.

~Address, Meeting with Asian Youth,
Dangjin, South Korea, August 15, 2014

Reflection: Time-lapse maps can show us the spread of civilizations or the rise of sea levels. Imagine if we could see the spread of spiritual deserts on those maps. How many people we know say that they are fine, but really are not?

We are made for God, and we suffer when we remove him from our lives, just as truly as we would if we stopped eating or drinking. Just as we are called to serve those who are physically starving in the world, we are called to bring Christ's living water to the world as well.

March 12

The Risk of Hope

CR

[HOPE] INVOLVES TAKING RISKS. It means being ready not to be seduced by what is fleeting, by false promises of happiness, by immediate and selfish pleasures, by a life of mediocrity and self-centeredness, which only fills the heart with sadness and bitterness.

No, hope is bold; it ... can open us up to grand ideals which make life more beautiful and worthwhile.

~Address to Students, Havana, Cuba,
September 20, 2015

Reflection: *Sic transit gloria mundi*: the glory of the world is short-lived. Even the greatest buildings of human hands have faded and decayed over time; many are in hard to reach places, and some are destroyed in war. Yet, people sacrificed their lives, their fortunes, their empires to build or acquire them.

Seeing things in the light of eternity—which never ever ends, and never ever fades—puts things in perspective. What couldn't I, wouldn't I, do to gain eternity? Eternity makes us all bold if we take it seriously.

March 13

Father of Lies

CR

IN THE BIBLE, the devil is called the father of lies. What he promises, or better, what he makes you think, is that if you do certain things, you will be happy. And later, when you think about it, you realize that you weren't happy at all.

~Address, Meeting with Young People,
Asunción, Paraguay, July 12, 2015

Reflection: It's so easy to get tricked by the devil into thinking things will make me happy that won't! What are some of the things I once thought would make me happy, but didn't? What are some of the things the devil wants me to think will make me happy now, but won't?

Reflecting on the difference between what *I* think will make me happy and what actually *does* satisfy me leads me to God and helps me outsmart the devil when he tempts me—but it means I have to pay attention! Do I recognize where my true happiness lies?

March 14

He Carries Our Cross with Us

CR

JESUS, WITH HIS CROSS, walks with us and takes upon himself our fears, our problems, and our sufferings, even those which are deepest and most painful.

[He says to us]: "Have courage! You do not carry your cross alone! I carry it with you. I have overcome death and I have come to give you hope, to give you life" (cf. Jn 3:16).

~Address, Way of the Cross,
Rio de Janiero, Brazil, July 26, 2013

Reflection: People sometimes refer to situations as being their cross—the thing that brings them suffering. And crosses do bring suffering. But when people wear crosses on their necks or hang them in their homes, they don't do this to remind us of death— quite the opposite!

Thanks to Jesus, our crosses also unite us: they unite us with him and with each other. We know that the cross is also a sign of resurrection. We Christians rejoice in the cross, despite the pain.

March 15

God Was in Love

☙

A YOUNG PERSON ONCE ASKED ME—you know how young people ask hard questions!—"Father, what did God do before he created the world?" Believe me, I had a hard time answering that one. I told him what I am going to tell you now.

Before he created the world, God was in love, because God is love. The love he had within himself, the love between the Father and the Son, in the Holy Spirit, was so great, so overflowing—I'm not sure if this is theologically precise, but you will get what I am saying—that love was so great that God could not be selfish.

He had to go out from himself, in order to have someone to love outside of himself. So God created the world.

~Address, Prayer Vigil, Philadelphia,
September 26, 2015

Reflection: When you are excited about some news that you have to tell, it's hard to keep it in. You may intend to tell people later, but instead you blurt it out right away. Your enthusiasm can't be contained!

God's love is like that: it's not just a feeling or a state of mind, it's almost like energy itself. This is the love that God has for us, and wants to give to us, for us to have, and for us to pass on. It is a gift that keeps on giving!

March 16

Let Us Respond

∞

IN YOUR CHRISTIAN LIVES, you will find many occasions that will tempt you ... to push away the stranger, the needy, the poor, and the brokenhearted. It is these people especially who repeat the cry of the woman of the Gospel: "Lord, help me!"

Let us respond, not like those who push away people who make demands on us, as if serving the needy gets in the way of our being close to the Lord. No! We are to be like Christ, who responds to every plea for his help with love, mercy, and compassion.

~Meeting with Asian Youth, Haemi Castle,
South Korea, August 17, 2014

Reflection: Many people want to be good. Many people want to serve—*their* way. One of the ways in which Christ challenges us is by asking us to love and serve him in ways we didn't plan and may not like.

When people we don't like or don't understand come to us with their needs, let's try to realize that Christ is coming to us through them, pushing us out of our comfort zones—and into his arms.

March 17

Let Peace Begin with Me

രു

NEVER FINISH THE DAY without making peace with one another. Listen to me carefully: Did you fight with your wife or husband? Kids—did you fight with your parents? Did you seriously argue? That's not a good thing, but it's not really that which is the problem: the problem arises only if this feeling hangs over into the next day.

So if you've fought, do not let the day end without making peace with your family. And how am I going to make peace? By getting down on my knees? No! Just by a small gesture, a little something, and harmony within your family will be restored....

Do you understand me? It's not easy, but you have to do it. It will help to make life so much more beautiful.

~General Audience, May 13, 2015

Reflection: All adults know that if you drink too much alcohol, the next day you don't feel good—you have a hangover. You may have a headache, feel sick to your stomach, and be especially tired. Most people avoid physical hangovers, because they're unpleasant.

Fighting leaves us with a different kind of hangover—we feel uncomfortable around people at home, a bit "off" inside. But we don't need to do a lot to end those personal hangovers with our family; we can make an effort to speak kindly to the people we fought with, we can give them a hug, we can get them a glass of water or something they need.

We may never stop fighting with our family members, but we can also keep fighting the ugly aftermath.

March 18

Nipping Bad Habits in the Bud

ভ

IT'S NOT ALWAYS EASY TO SAY [pardon me, and I'm sorry], but it is so necessary. Whenever it is lacking, the little cracks begin to open up—even when we don't want them to—and they can even become enormous sinkholes.

~General Audience, May 13, 2015

Reflection: Most bad habits start small. Not apologizing is one of them. It's so easy to find excuses, especially since we can usually find some way of blaming the other person. We tell ourselves, "She started it." Or, "I'll apologize *if* … " And so we never look at the damage we've done, and the things we could—and should—be truly sorry for.

Week after week, year after year, the weight of our bad habits takes its toll. Our loved ones don't feel so loved anymore. Fighting those bad habits can take great faith: the faith to trust that even a small step is a big one, and taking that step.

March 19

A Man of Faith

Feast of St. Joseph, Husband of the Blessed Virgin Mary

◌

[ST.] JOSEPH WAS ... FIRST AND FOREMOST ... A MAN OF FAITH. Faith gave Joseph the power to find light just at the moment when everything seemed dark. Faith sustained him amid the troubles of life. Thanks to faith, Joseph was able to press forward when everything seemed to be holding him back.

In the face of unjust and painful situations, faith brings us the light which scatters the darkness. As it did for Joseph, faith makes us open to the quiet presence of God at every moment of our lives, in every person, and in every situation.

~Greeting, Charitable Center, St. Patrick Parish,
Washington, D.C., September 24, 2015

Reflection: The life that St. Joseph lived was not an easy one. Called to be an earthly father to Jesus, he was unable to find a good place for Jesus to be born, and, then, after Jesus' birth, he had to flee with his family to Egypt and live there to escape death threats. He went through a lot.

We don't know much about him and his life, but we know that at certain critical moments an angel visited him to help him understand what to do. He was a man of action, but he was also a man of deep trust and great attention: He listened and obeyed. Even in times of hardship and anxiety, he had faith that the Lord was with him. This is what made him such a great father, and such a great saint.

March 20

Doing What the Lord Commands—
Without Knowing the Details

CR

As MARY BIDS US, let us "do what the Lord tells us." Do what he tells you. And let us be thankful that in this, our time and our hour, the new wine, the finest wine, will make us recover the joy of families, the joy of living in a family. Let it be so.

~Homily, Mass for Families,
Guayaquil, Ecuador, July 6, 2015

Reflection: When Mary told the servants to do whatever Jesus told them, she didn't know his plan. But she trusted him and knew he would do something good.

Let's follow Jesus that same way: not expecting to know all the details of everything in every second, but knowing that he can recover the joy of our family life if we are willing to do what he tells us.

March 21

We Can All Do Our Part

℣

"CHILDREN, OBEY YOUR PARENTS in everything, for this pleases the Lord. Fathers, do not provoke your children, lest they become discouraged" (Col 3:20-21). This is a wise rule: children should be raised to listen to their parents and obey their parents, who, in turn, should not order them around in a negative way, so as not to discourage the children.

~General Audience, May 20, 2015

Reflection: When we hear this reading from St. Paul at Mass with our families, a lot of people give each other looks—or they want to. We think, "See, you are supposed to obey us!" or "See, you aren't supposed to nag us!" We all need to be reminded of our own responsibilities in making family life better.

We are *all* called to love more truly in the way we treat one another, and we need reminders. We need to listen, and to stay focused on the positive—we all need to keep our eyes on the prize.

March 22

The Great Gift of Friendship

ॐ

FRIENDSHIP IS ONE OF THE GREATEST GIFTS which a person, a young person, can have and can offer. It really is. How hard it is to live without friends!

Think about it: isn't that one of the most beautiful things that Jesus tells us? He says, "I have called you friends, for all that I have heard from my Father I have made known to you" (Jn 15:15).

~Address, Meeting with Young People,
Asunción, Paraguay, July 12, 2015

Reflection: Having a true friend is a precious gift: if you have a great friend, you already know this! But finding great friends isn't always easy—and many times they come in an unexpected way. If Jesus called us his friends, surely it is important to him that we value our friendships.

Is there a way I can reach out to someone in friendship—to someone who is already my friend or who might want to be? Jesus wants us to be—and to have—friends; he communicates with us through them. Can I be a better listener with my friends?

March 23

Caring for the Body and the Soul

CR

WE ARE ALWAYS QUITE MOVED when we see images of sick and malnourished children that are shown in so many parts of the world.

At the same time, we are also deeply moved by the twinkle in the eyes of many children, deprived of everything and in schools built from nothing, who are proud when showing off their pencil and their notebook. And how lovingly they look at their teacher!

Children already know that man does not live on bread alone!

~General Audience, June 3, 2015

Reflection: Being bathed, clothed, and fed is a wonderful thing. And yet we don't just *want* more than this in life; we *need* more. That need is for more than any human person could ever satisfy.

We can love each other better if we recognize that need for more and respond to it in the ways we can: by just spending time with someone, by listening when they speak, or remembering what is important to them.

None of us were made for bread alone; let's be loving and patient with each other in those needs—even if we cannot fully satisfy them.

March 24

Our Job Is Taking Care of Families

CR

WE CHRISTIANS HAVE TO BE EVER CLOSER to the families whom poverty puts to the test. But think, all of you know someone: a father without work, a mother without work ... and this makes the family suffer, the bonds are weakened. This is terrible.... Take care of families ... when destitution puts the family to the test!

~General Audience, June 3, 2015

Reflection: It's more difficult to be kind and patient when you're hungry and tired. All parents of young children grow afraid of the "witching hours" before dinner when parents are tired and children are whiny, and everyone is hungry and short-tempered. Even some of the calmest mothers have a hard time being gentle at that time of day!

When someone is out of work or other difficult circumstances hit a family, everyone suffers; the stress can put everyone on edge. Sometimes people try to suffer silently, because they are embarrassed to admit their difficulties. But we can learn to be sensitive to people, to their pain, and their humiliation.

We can be attentive to our own families, and to other families we know. Let's look for ways we can take care of each other—in difficult hours and in difficult years.

March 25

God Sent His Son to a Family

☙

WHEN THE MAN AND HIS WIFE WENT ASTRAY and walked away from God, God did not leave them alone. Such was his love. So great was his love that he began to walk with mankind, he began to walk alongside his people, until the right time came, and then he gave the greatest demonstration of love: his Son.

And where did he send his Son? To a palace, to a city, to an office building? He sent him to a family.

~Address, Prayer Vigil, Philadelphia,
September 26, 2015

Reflection: At the beginning of creation, God made a grown man and a grown woman. That man and woman made mistakes and went away from God, but he kept loving them. And when he decided to come to earth to join us, he didn't start over with a completely new plan, something other than man and woman—he had gotten his creation right the first time!

But this time it was the baby who came first, to a chosen woman and man. A baby who was God himself. But in giving that God-baby to a regular human family, he reminds us that the family, despite all our mistakes, is still the place he arrives first.

March 26

Everyday Heroes

ଔ

IN THE FACE OF ILLNESS, even in families, difficulties arise due to human weakness. But in general, times of illness enable family bonds to grow stronger....

How often do we see a man or woman arrive at work with a weary face ... and, when we ask them "What happened?" they answer: "I only slept two hours because we are taking turns at home to be close to our boy, our girl, our sick one, our grandfather, our grandmother." And the day of work goes on.

These are heroic deeds, the heroism of families! That hidden heroism carried out with tenderness and courage when someone at home is sick.

~General Audience, June 10, 2015

Reflection: Everybody wants to be a hero. But being a hero isn't always exciting or glamorous—taking care of people when they are sick can be very hard! It helps to remember, though, that in these small daily acts our true character—and our true heroism—come through. As Jesus said, whoever is faithful to me in small things will also be faithful in greater ones.

Lord, give us the strength and love to be heroes in everyday matters!

March 27

Turning Conflict into an Opportunity

CR

WE MAKE MISTAKES, YES; we have problems, yes. But we know that that is not really what counts. We know that mistakes, problems, and conflicts are an opportunity to draw closer to others, to draw closer to God.

~Address, Prayer Vigil, Philadelphia,
September 26, 2015

Reflection: A strange thing often happens when we take tests: We tend to remember our mistakes more than anything else. We remember what we did wrong (and, hopefully, we now remember or have figured out the correct answer!).

Mistakes and conflicts happen a lot in our lives with other people. This can discourage us, or it can be an opportunity to realize that our God isn't so interested in our mistakes: he is more interested in what we remember, now; what we choose to focus on *now.*

Lord, let me remember that you are present.

March 28

Just a Small Step

CR

WE ARE ALL SINNERS, needing to be purified by the Lord. But it is enough to take a small step towards Jesus to realize that he awaits us always with open arms, particularly in the Sacrament of Reconciliation.

~Message for the Thirtieth World Youth Day, 2015

Reflection: Some people think that recognizing our sinfulness leads to guilt and feeling overwhelmed by that guilt. But recognizing our sin is the first step to healing—it's like calling a disease by its name. And then we can take steps toward purification.

Can I make a habit of regular confession? If I haven't been recently, when can I go next?

Lord, help me to seek and find you in the Sacrament of Reconciliation!

March 29

Are You Ready?

☙

DEAR YOUNG FRIENDS, in this generation, the Lord is counting on you! He is counting on you! He entered your hearts on the day of your baptism; he gave you his Spirit on the day of your confirmation; and he strengthens you constantly by his presence in the Eucharist, so that you can be his witnesses before the world. Are you ready to say "yes"? Are you ready?

~Address, Meeting with Asian Youth,
Dangjin, South Korea, August 15, 2014

Reflection: There is a famous poster from the World War II era that shows a picture of an older man—Uncle Sam—pointing his finger. The caption reads, "I want you (for the U.S. Army)." He seems to be pointing at the person looking at the poster.

It's the same with the Lord. He has plans for each of us. He needs YOU! Are you—are we—ready?

March 30

Patience and Forgiveness

ϾᎡ

FATHERS MUST BE PATIENT. Often there is nothing else to do but wait, pray, and wait with patience, gentleness, magnanimity, and mercy.

A good father *knows how to wait and knows how to forgive* from the depths of his heart.

~General Audience, February 4, 2015

Reflection: We know that waiting is useful, even if we hate to wait. If people are angry, we may ask them to wait before they act so that they can cool off. We put angry children in timeouts to get them to calm down. Waiting helps us gain perspective, too, and so it helps us to forgive. The extra time that it takes to deal with children or angry people gives us more time to accept and forgive.

When we have to wait, can we try to see what our waiting can teach us?

March 31

Called to Speak His Name

CR

WE DISCIPLES OF THE LORD have a further mission: that of being "channels" that pass on Jesus' love. And in this mission you, teenagers and young people, play a special role: You are called to speak about Jesus to your peers....

This is a commitment especially reserved to you, because with your courage, your enthusiasm, spontaneity, and ease of getting together, you are more easily able to reach the mind and heart of those who have distanced themselves from the Lord.

So many teenagers and young people your age have an immense need of someone who through their own life tells them that Jesus knows us, that Jesus loves us, that Jesus forgives us, shares our difficulties with us, and supports us with his grace.

~Address to German Altar Servers,
Rome, August 5, 2014

Reflection: If you had a friend who was sick and you knew of something that would cure him, would you tell him? Even if the medicine tasted weird or it had to be taken many times a day? Of course you would!

Sometimes, religious people forget that Jesus really heals us. We forget all we have to be grateful for. Since our wounds and problems haven't magically disappeared, we forget that we are on a road to recovery nonetheless. But it *is* a road to recovery, and Jesus wants us all to walk it.

We need to know when and how to say things to our friends intelligently, in a way that reaches and respects them. But let's not be afraid—and let's not forget to be grateful for all God has done in our lives.

April 1

Hope Is More than Optimism

ॐ

WHAT IS HOPE? Does it mean being optimistic? No. Optimism is a state of mind. Tomorrow, you wake up in a bad mood and you're not optimistic at all; you see everything in a bad light.

Hope is something more. Hope involves suffering. Hope can accept suffering as part of building something; it is able to sacrifice. Are you able to sacrifice for the future, or do you simply want to live for the day and let those yet to come fend for themselves?

~Address to Students, Havana, Cuba,
September 20, 2015

Reflection: Ever hear people talk about whether the glass is half empty or hall full? Hope isn't about this. The glass can be completely empty or completely full, but you know that there is a hand that pours the glass for you. That is Christian hope.

We know that our greatest thirst is for Someone real, and who has already come for us. Hope is much greater than optimism, because it doesn't depend on my mood or my state of mind: We can suffer—and even die—knowing that life is still good.

Lord, give me your hope—the hope that didn't die even on the cross!

April 2

Made to Listen

ℭ℞

WE ARE MADE to listen to one another and help one another.
~General Audience, April 15, 2015

Reflection: When it comes to our five senses, we sometimes have more than one word to explain what we do. We can see without watching. We can hear without listening. To listen means to hear and to pay attention. Just as our ears and our minds are made for this, our soul is, too.

Really listening—paying attention to someone—is a huge gift. If we really listen, we almost can't avoid helping each other, because when our heart is in the right place, action follows.

Lord, give me ears to hear—and listen!

April 3

Blessed Are the Poor

ℭ

LET US NOT FORGET that this is the first of the beatitudes: "Blessed are the poor in spirit," those who are not attached to riches, to the powers of this world.

~Homily, Vespers, Havana, Cuba,
September 20, 2015

Reflection: Jesus tells us that he is the way, the truth, and the life. Being poor in spirit is part of living in the truth. It's not a lack of self-esteem or a lack of money that defines poverty of spirit. It's humility in front of life and gratitude for all that is given, because everything we have is from God.

Being poor in spirit prevents us from being attached to the powers of this world and focuses us instead on the powers of the next, which are much more enduring and powerful.

April 4

The Grace to Forgive

ॐ

EACH DAY, IN THE WORDS OF THE OUR FATHER, we ask God to forgive us and to grant us the grace to forgive others. As difficult as forgiveness may be, it is essential for our personal growth, our capacity to acknowledge our failures and to mend broken relationships. It is a virtue we learn first in the family.

~General Audience, November 4, 2015

Reflection: In the Our Father, we ask God for our daily bread. The part about forgiving and being forgiven comes next, since it's a daily sort of thing: every day I sin; every day someone sins against me.

It makes it a lot easier to forgive if I remember first how much I've been forgiven; that I've been loved in spite of my flaws. When I don't know how to forgive, I can at least pray that I can learn. It's right there, in the Our Father.

April 5

Jesus Doesn't Lie

CR

JESUS DOESN'T LIE TO US. He shows us a path which is life and truth. He is the great proof of this. His style, his way of living, is friendship, relationship with his Father. And that is what he offers us. He makes us realize that we are sons and daughters. Beloved children.

~Address, Meeting with Young People, Asunción, Paraguay, July 12, 2015

Reflection: Sometimes, being a parent or a child feels like a lot of work. There is a lot to do in a household, and sometimes parents feel like managing it is a full-time job.

Children often feel the burden of their responsibilities, too; it is easy for everyone to lose the bigger picture of the love and joy that God intended for family life.

But that is what he wants for us: that all parents should know that they are his beloved children, whatever their mistakes, and that their children should feel the same, knowing that their parents' love is real, true, and a reflection of our heavenly Father's love.

That loving relationship came first, before all of the work of family life; and all that work rests on a solid foundation of love.

Do I know I am a beloved child of God?

April 6

Let Him Look

ᚺ

IT IS MORE DIFFICULT to allow God to look at *us* than [for *us*] to look at God ... because we always resist. [God] waits for us, he looks at us, he always seeks us.

~Address, Visit with Detainees,
Castrovillari, Italy, June 21, 2014

Reflection: Most people don't like the idea of being on camera or videotaped without knowing: it's embarrassing. We don't like what we look like or what we do, and we don't want others to see and know.

We have a hard time letting God look at us for similar reasons. We have many images of what we should be like, and allowing God to see us pierces our self-image. But he made us—he already knows!

Can we allow him to look at us so that we can see ourselves more truly? Instead of resisting him, can we try to understand how he sees?

April 7

Wise Use of Our Time

CR

OUR LIFE IS MADE OF TIME, and time is God's gift…. Perhaps many teenagers and young people waste too much time…: *chatting* on the internet or on mobile phones, watching … TV, technological progress that should simplify and improve the quality of life, but sometimes distract you from what is really important.

~Address to German Altar Servers,
Rome, August 5, 2014

Reflection: Once, when people complained about things that Jesus did on the Sabbath, he asked, "Was man made for the Sabbath, or was the Sabbath made for man?" And similarly we can ask, "Was technology made for us, or were we made for it?"

Technology is a great gift; it is greatly useful—but the key is that we have to use *it,* not the other way around. Otherwise, we become slaves to our technological devices. We can use our phones and televisions to teach us things, enjoy time with other people, and stay close to them when they are far away. Or we can use them to distract us, to avoid each other, to waste our time so that we don't face difficult situations.

We need to pause from time to time and think about how we use our devices. What about me: am I master or slave in my relationship to technology? And do I use my time wisely, recognizing the great gift that it is?

April 8

Natural and Supernatural Love

ରେ

CHILDREN ARE LOVED BEFORE THEY ARRIVE. So often I find mothers in the square who are expecting a baby and ask me for a blessing ... these babies are loved before coming into the world.

And this is free, this is love; they are loved before being born, like the love of God who always loves us first. They are loved before having done anything to deserve it, before knowing how to talk or think, even before coming into the world!

~General Audience, February 11, 2015

Reflection: No one can love us like God does, but they can help reveal his face. The love of a mother for her child is natural, but it helps us understand the supernatural. When parents find out they are having a child, they get excited. They look at sonograms and often share the images with their family and friends.

It almost seems crazy for parents to be excited and happy about a child they don't yet *know*—yet that is how God wanted it from the beginning. Do we realize how extraordinary this is—how much we are loved? And yet, our natural experience is just a shadow, helping lead us to him and his eternal, extravagant love.

April 9

Free but Never Alone

℘

WE CAN LEARN THE GOOD RELATIONSHIP between generations from our heavenly Father, who leaves each of us free but never leaves us on our own. And if we err, he continues to follow us with patience, without abating his love for us.

Our heavenly Father does not take steps back in his love for us, ever! He always goes forward, and if he cannot go forward, he waits for us, but he never goes backward; he wants his children to be brave and take their steps forward.

~General Audience, February 11, 2015

Reflection: So many times in life, it seems as if we make progress in something, but then we slide backward again. We slip into bad habits, lose our tempers, or just quit trying.

One of the mysteries of God is how he continues loving us and standing by us, whether we're up or down. Which means that even when slipping, if we turn to him, we can always make progress in our ability to trust him. He waits for us. So however far backward we've slid, we can always still go forward with God.

April 10

Humbly Building a New World

ଓ

CHILDREN, FOR THEIR PART, must not be afraid of the task of building a new world: it is right for them to want to improve on what they have received! But this must be done without arrogance.

~General Audience, February 11, 2015

Reflection: Wanting to build a new world is a beautiful thing! It shows energy, passion, and desire—and a willingness to work to make life better. But we need to start by recognizing all that is already around us and all that has already been built.

Families are a great place for grounding us: Young people who dream and want to build can share their enthusiasm with older, wiser parents and grandparents who understand the efforts and history of what has gone before.

This way, the young can pass on their hopes to the old and prevent them from being cynical. The old can share their experience with the young and keep them from being naive and ungrateful.

Lord, help us learn virtue and perspective by listening to each other!

April 11

Jesus Cleans Our Wounds

CR

WE ARE ALL WOUNDED, in one way or another. And so we bring our wounds to the wounds of Jesus. Why? So that there they can be soothed, washed clean, changed, and healed.

He died for us, for me, so that he could stretch out us his hand and lift us up.... Jesus wants to help you get up, always.

~Address, Rehabilitation Center,
Santa Cruz de la Sierra, Bolivia, July 10, 2015

Reflection: Before modern antibiotics, more people died from the infections caused by their wounds than from the wounds themselves. It's not just being hurt that kills us; it's all the ugly ways that our wounds get infected and ugly—just like the ways we've been hurt or mistreated can make us mean and ugly to one another.

Even if our wounds remain, cleaning them is a big step toward healing. Admitting that we've been hurt and allowing someone to help clean our wounds is a big step toward spiritual healing.

April 12

Mary, Jesus' Gift

CR

THE VIRGIN MARY, MOTHER OF GOD AND OUR MOTHER ... is the gift that Jesus gives to his people.... Mary has always been, and will always be, with her children, especially the poor and those most in need.

~Angelus, July 12, 2015

Reflection: One of the last things Jesus did on the cross was to give two of the people he loved most in the world to each other: the apostle John and his mother Mary. As he was dying, he gave John a new mother, and Mary a new son. Mary wasn't just Jesus' mother anymore, but everyone's.

Mary was always poor because she knew that everything came from God and not herself. But her poverty was her greatness, because she accepted everything from God and gave everything to him.

Whenever we realize our own poverty, we can beg Mary to intercede for us. Virgin Mother, help me to accept my poverty and weakness as the surest way to your Son.

April 13

Jesus Washes Our Feet

ଔ

I THINK OF THE GOSPEL SCENE where Jesus washes the feet of his disciples at the Last Supper. This was something his disciples found hard to accept. Even Peter refused, and told him: "You will never wash my feet" (Jn 13:8)....

We also know in faith that Jesus seeks us out. He wants to heal our wounds, to soothe our feet which hurt from traveling alone, to wash each of us clean of the dust from our journey. He doesn't ask us where we have been, he doesn't question us about what we have done. Rather, he tells us, "Unless I wash your feet, you have no share with me" (Jn 13:8).

Unless I wash your feet, I will not be able to give you the life which the Father always dreamed of, the life for which he created you. Jesus comes to meet us so that he can restore our dignity as children of God. He wants to help us to set out again, to resume our journey, to recover our hope, to restore our faith and trust.

~Address, Visit to Detainees, Philadelphia,
September 27, 2015

Reflection: If you ask people to tell you their best feature, hardly anyone would say their feet. They smell; they're often ugly; they get dry skin, callouses, bunions, and ingrown nails; and, if you walk around barefoot, they get really dirty, too. Many people are uncomfortable letting others see their feet.

But this is what Jesus longs to do: to clean and heal us in all the ugliest and most embarrassing and dirtiest places of ourselves. But we're afraid, because we know it means letting Jesus into places we're not proud of. Do we want the life that the Father has dreamed of for us? Or do we want the petty, dirty, little life that we're capable of on our own—*and* stinky feet?

April 14

Will You Help Him Carry the Cross?

 C౪

TODAY I ASK YOU.... Do you want to be like Pilate, who did not have the courage to go against the tide to save Jesus' life, and instead washed his hands?

Tell me: Are you one of those who wash their hands, who feign ignorance and look the other way? Or are you like Simon of Cyrene, who helped Jesus to carry that heavy wood, or like Mary and the other women, who were not afraid to accompany Jesus all the way to the end, with love and tenderness?

And you, who do you want to be? Like Pilate? Like Simon? Like Mary? Jesus is looking at you now and is asking you: Do you want to help me carry the cross?

~Address, Way of the Cross,
Rio de Janeiro, Brazil, July 26, 2013

Reflection: Life is full of awkward moments and uncomfortable situations, difficult choices and painful requests. Christ is coming to us in those moments, asking us, "Will you look at me and follow me, or would you rather stay safe and comfortable?"

At the end of time, it is the suffering ones who will be consoled and comforted—not the comfortable. He wants us to choose a grand and beautiful way, not an easy one. If we're afraid, that's OK—he will give us the courage to sustain us.

Lord, give me the strength to look, not look away.

April 15

He Shares Every Cross

CR

THERE IS NO CROSS, BIG OR SMALL, in our life, which the Lord does not share with us.

~Address, Way of the Cross,
Rio de Janeiro, Brazil, July 26, 2013

Reflection: God is with us. And God is good—all the time. When a cross seems too strange or too great to bear, remember this. He is always with us, until the end of time.

April 16

Learning to Stand at the Cross

CR

THE DISCIPLES WERE AFRAID TO QUESTION JESUS when he spoke to them about his passion and death. He frightened them; they could not grasp the thought of seeing Jesus suffer on the cross.

We too are tempted to flee from our own crosses and those of others, to withdraw from those who suffer....

Let us now lift our gaze to the Virgin Mary, our Mother [and] ... ask her to teach us to stand beside the cross of our brothers and sisters who suffer.

~Angelus, September 20, 2015

Reflection: When someone is hurt and we can help him or her, we often do. But when someone is suffering and we don't know what to do, most of the time we turn away. Watching their pain often feels too hard.

Mary never left her Son while he was carrying his cross and dying on it. She couldn't do anything to help him, but she stayed with him. We can learn from her how to love people when they're suffering and how, by looking at her Son, we can find the strength not to turn away

April 17

A House Divided

ॐ

THE DEVIL WANTS YOU TO QUARREL among yourselves, because in this way he divides you, he defeats you, and he robs you of faith.

~Address, Visit to the People of Bañado
Norte, Asunción, Paraguay, July 12, 2015

Reflection: The devil is tricky. If he sees you're against him, he'll try to get you on his side by messing with you in little things. He'll try to distract you so that you don't notice what he's doing.

This is what often happens when we argue. How many times we get into big fights—and then can't even remember what they were about! There are times when we need to discuss things—and we don't always agree—but let's pray for the grace to recognize when an argument is simply a temptation and a trick of the devil.

Lord, show me what you need me to say, and need me to hear. Do not let me get caught in the devil's snares of pointless arguments.

April 18

No Excuses

❧

I REMEMBER, WHEN I WAS VISITING A RETIREMENT HOME, I spoke with each person and I frequently heard this: "How are you? And your children? Well, well. How many do you have? Many. And do they come to visit you? Oh sure, yes, always, yes, they come. When was the last time they came?" I remember an elderly woman who said to me: "Mmm, for Christmas."

It was August! Eight months without being visited by her children, abandoned for eight months!

This is called mortal sin. Understand?

~General Audience, March 4, 2015

Reflection: We live in a world that uses people a lot. Sometimes we think that's okay, or that's just how things are—but that's nothing more than an excuse. Not to visit people when they are old and lonely (especially our own family members!) is wrong. Let's not make excuses.

April 19

Do as I Say—or as I Do?

 App

ONCE, AS A CHILD, a grandmother told us the story of an old grandfather who got dirty while eating because he couldn't easily bring the spoonful of soup to his mouth. And his son, that is, the father of the family, had decided to move him from the dinner table and set up a little table in the kitchen to eat alone, so he couldn't be seen. In this way he wouldn't make a bad impression when friends came over to lunch or dinner.

A few days later, he came home and found his youngest child playing with some wood and a hammer and nails, he was making something there, he said: "What are you making?" — "I'm making a table, papa."—"A table, why?"—"To have one for when you grow old, so that you can eat there."

~General Audience, March 4, 2015

Reflection: Our children see the way we treat others, especially the elderly and the needy. This sometimes helps us understand—even in a painful way—where we have gone wrong. There is very little that escapes our children's attention. Knowing that we are teaching by our actions can help us be aware of, and then correct, our mistakes.

It should also inspire us: When we treat our family members with patience, humility, and affection, we are building a foundation of love for the next generation as well.

April 20

The Lord Needs You

CR

TODAY ... AS ALWAYS, THE LORD NEEDS YOU, young people, for his Church. My friends, the Lord needs you! Today ... he is calling each of you to follow him in his Church and to be missionaries. The Lord is calling you today! Not the masses, but you, and you, and you, each one of you. Listen to what he is saying to you in your heart.

~Address, Prayer Vigil, Rio de Janeiro,
Brazil, July 27, 2013

Reflection: You. The Lord is calling *you*. In English we have just one word for "you," but some languages have more: some distinguish between people you know more formally and those you know more intimately; many distinguish between the singular and plural you.

When the Lord calls you, he is using the singular, informal you—let there be no mistake. He knows you and wants you *specifically*. The relationship he wants with you is deeply, intimately personal. Listen for him.

April 21

The Devil Doesn't Deliver

ભ

THE DEVIL IS A CON ARTIST. He makes promises after promise, but he never delivers. He'll never really do anything he says. He doesn't make good on his promises. He makes you want things which he can't give … [to] put your hopes in things which will never make you happy. That's his game, his strategy. He talks a lot, he offers a lot, but he doesn't deliver.

~Address, Meeting with Young People,
Asunción, Paraguay, July 12, 2015

Reflection: The first commandment reminds us not to worship idols, because there is only one true God, and "he brought us out of slavery"—he delivers!

Following the devil is like worshiping idols, because he might seem like a god, but he's not—and you can tell by the way he operates. He promises us power, but makes us his slaves; he never actually gives us any of the happiness he promises: it's always tomorrow.

Thank God that we can choose not to be the devil's slaves! Let us give thanks, today, that we get to make that choice, and make it wholeheartedly.

April 22

Grandparents' Gift of Prayer

℘

THE PRAYER OF GRANDPARENTS and of the elderly is a great gift for the Church; it is a treasure! A great injection of wisdom for the whole of human society.

~General Audience, March 11, 2015

Reflection: When children are young, their parents can easily lose perspective on things. One of the great gifts of grandparents is perspective. They have seen their children grow up—they've grown up enough to have children of their own. So they love their grandchildren, but they also understand more naturally how much life is in God's hands.

Lord, help parents and grandparents to always pray for their children!

April 23

God Always Has the Upper Hand

ᘓ

I WOULD LIKE TO SAY FORCEFULLY: Always know in your heart that God is by your side; he never abandons you! Let us never lose hope! Let us never allow it to die in our hearts! The "dragon," evil, is present in our history, but it does not have the upper hand.

The one with the upper hand is God, and God is our hope!

~Homily, Shrine of Our Lady of Aparecida,
Brazil, July 24, 2013

Reflection: When we see images of St. George or St. Michael the Archangel, they are usually shown defeating a dragon. Some images of Mary will also show her stepping on and crushing the head of a serpent. The dragons and serpents symbolize the devil, the presence of evil.

At times, it seems like evil has taken over the world: terrorism, school shootings, economic hardship … people everywhere are suffering every day. But the idea that evil has won is itself a temptation. The idea that the darkness is more powerful than God is one of the ways that evil enters our hearts: we stop believing; we give up.

Let us never forget that we worship a God who has crushed evil. Evil is still present in our world, but it will never, ever win. Let's not let it win our hearts.

April 24

The Grace and Vocation of Old Age

☙

THE LORD NEVER DISCARDS [THE ELDERLY]. He calls us to follow him in every age of life, and *old age has a grace and a mission*, too, a true vocation from the Lord. Old age is a vocation. It is not yet time to "pull in the oars."

This period of life is different from those before, there is no doubt; we even have to somewhat "invent it ourselves," because our societies are not ready ... to appreciate the true value of this stage of life.

~General Audience, March 12, 2015

Reflection: I heard about a woman who started taking piano lessons at age sixty. Some people laughed—why bother at that age? But she's ninety now, and she's a concert pianist. Our societies may not yet realize the potential in the lives of the elderly, but we can as individuals.

God has a plan for us—different perhaps from the plan of the earlier part of our lives, but no less rich and important. Let us have the courage to recognize that the adventure of life is not over, even in our later years.

April 25

Making Himself Understood by Children

CR

IT IS CURIOUS: God has no difficulty in making himself understood by children, and children have no difficulty in understanding God. It is not by chance that in the Gospel there are several very beautiful and powerful words of Jesus regarding the "little ones."

~General Audience, March 18, 2015

Reflection: There are some teachings of our faith that can be hard to understand—such as the Trinity. But these truths are hard for everyone, not just children! Many times, we think that kids cannot understand things. But Christianity is an experience available to everyone, at any age or stage of life.

It is the nature of mysteries that although we understand them incompletely, we can enter into them more and more over time. Children often have an easier time accepting this challenge than adults do.

Lord, give us the grace to understand as children do, and give us the grace to express your truth in ways everyone can understand.

April 26

Help!

ℭЯ

WE ALL ARE IN NEED OF HELP, of love, and of forgiveness!
~General Audience, March 18, 2015

Reflection: Most of the time when Pope Francis speaks in front an audience, he asks the people to pray for him. Pope Francis needs our help—he needs our prayers. If the pope needs us so much, and isn't afraid to tell us, how can we be afraid to recognize how much help we all need?

Lord, help me to realize that needing help is a good thing!

April 27

On Angels' Wings

GR

ON THE JOURNEY AND IN THE TRIALS OF LIFE we are not alone, we are accompanied and sustained by the angels of God, who offer, so to speak, their wings to help us overcome the many dangers, to be able to fly above those [things] that can make our lives difficult or drag us down.

~Address, Blessing of the Statue of
St. Michael, Vatican Gardens, July 5, 2013

Reflection: Throughout history, people saw birds and dreamed of flying. Many inventors experimented more or less unsuccessfully. But then, in the early twentieth century, with the invention of airplanes, human flight became a reality.

We don't know much about angels, but we always picture them with wings: we know they can bring us above and beyond things we are incapable of, and that they can bring us to God. They are God's messengers: Let us call on them when we cannot see our way around the dangers and difficulties we face.

April 28

He Sees Beyond Appearances

༼༽

JESUS' LOVE GOES BEFORE US; his look anticipates our needs. He can see beyond appearances, beyond sin, beyond failures and unworthiness....

He sees beyond all of this. He sees our dignity as sons and daughters, a dignity at times sullied by sin, but one which endures in the depth of our soul.

~Homily, Mass, Holguín, Cuba,
September 21, 2015

Reflection: Many people clean up *before* they have a cleaning service come to their house. Often, they are embarrassed to let someone else see how they live. They want to fix things up before they'll let people come in.

God knows how we live, and he loves us anyway. He sees the grime of our sin, but knows we're much more than that. The question is whether we'll let him in so he can clean house in our souls.

April 29

His Word Gives Life—Every Day

☙

THE WORD OF GOD MAKES THINGS GROW, it gives life. And here, I would like to remind you once again, of the importance of having the Gospel, the Bible, close at hand—a small [copy of the] Gospel in your purse, in your pocket and to nourish yourselves every day with this living Word of God.

Read a passage from the Gospel every day, a passage from the Bible. Please don't ever forget this. Because this is the power that makes the life of the kingdom of God sprout within us.

~Angelus, June 14, 2015

Reflection: If you go into a hotel in the United States, you'll almost always find a Bible in the bedside table drawer. There are free apps for reading the Bible in many different translations, Bibles that can fit in a pocket or purse. There are Bibles of every size and shape for sale in bookstores and for free online.

Have I read anything from the Bible today? If not, what am I waiting for?

April 30
Relearning Tenderness

 C&

CHILDREN—IN THEIR INTERIOR SIMPLICITY—bring with them the capacity to receive and give tenderness. Tenderness is having a heart "of flesh" and not "of stone," as the Bible says (cf. Ez 36:26). Tenderness is also poetry: it is "feeling" things and events, not treating them as mere objects, only to use them.

~General Audience, March 18, 2015

Reflection: It often seems like part of growing up is growing "harder"—not letting ourselves feel things as strongly as we did when we were children. It can be difficult to face some of the challenging experiences of life without becoming hardened; it's actually more difficult to face them with tender hearts.

But this is what we are called to do, because it's only in this way that we can look at the world and its people with compassion, not as objects to use or obstacles to overcome.

Lord, don't let us grow hardened by our experience. Give us the tenderness and compassion of your Sacred Heart.

May 1

God's Call—and His Push

ଔ

GOD'S PRESENCE IN OUR LIVES never leaves us tranquil: it always pushes to do something. When God comes, he always calls us out of our house.

We are visited so that we can visit others; we are encountered so as to encounter others; we receive love in order to give love.

~Homily, Mass, Santiago, Cuba, September 22, 2015

Reflection: There is a restlessness that comes from not having God in our lives. We get bored easily, we move from one thing to the next in search of a satisfaction that never comes.

But there is another kind of restlessness that comes from God's presence. We've been given so much—we have to share it! Knowing that we are called, we are moved by the need to answer him. God starts a process in motion that we are compelled to continue.

May 2

Life with Children: Cheer Amid the Challenges

ର

CHILDREN BRING LIFE, CHEERFULNESS, HOPE, also troubles. But such is life. Certainly, they also bring worries and sometimes many problems; but better a society with these worries and these problems than a sad, gray society because it is without children!

~General Audience, March 18, 2015

Reflection: When I was a child, I was aware that I lived in a household where my things got lost and destroyed easily. My siblings would steal my toys and rip the heads off my Barbies. So, sometimes, when I got a present in tight packaging, I wouldn't open it. That way, I explained to my mother, the pieces couldn't get ruined and lost. This was true, but I also couldn't play with my gift!

Sometimes, our desire for peace and order gets in the way of our greater and deeper desire for joy. Children—our own and other people's—are a reminder that joy is truer and greater than our troubles; and that the truest order in life comes from the Lord.

May 3
Never Abandoned

CR

THE CHURCH, AS A MOTHER, never abandons the family, even when it is downhearted, wounded, and humiliated in so many ways. Neither when it falls into sin nor moves away from the Church; she will always do everything to try to care for and heal it, to call it to conversion, and to reconcile it to the Lord.

~General Audience, March 25, 2015

Reflection: Biologically, when a woman has a child, the child is always hers. That can never be undone, whatever happens.

This is true of the Church with her children as well. No matter what we do or where we stray, we are the Church's children, and she always beckons us to come back to her. But just like an ordinary mother with her beloved child, she likes it when we stay close, and sometimes we need to tell her what we need.

May 4

Finding the Strength We Don't Have

ଔ

AT TIMES ... THE HEART NO LONGER FINDS the strength to love.... But it is precisely in the darkness that Christ lights the fire of God's love: a flash breaks through the darkness and announces a new start.

~General Audience, April 1, 2015

Reflection: Sometimes, loving people is very difficult—especially (though not only) when you live with them! Sometimes, the worst part is feeling like you don't even want to try.

God knows this, and it is in moments like these—when we are too tired, frustrated, or sad to love—that we can pray, we can beg Christ to give us his love. He never withholds anything good, and he doesn't fail us when we ask him.

May 5

Love Is a Promise

CR

TO WANT TO FORM A FAMILY is to resolve to be a part of God's dream, to choose to dream with him, to want to build with him, to join him in this saga of building a world where no one will feel alone, unwanted, or homeless.

As Christians, we appreciate the beauty of the family and of family life as the place where we come to learn the meaning and value of human relationships. We learn that "to love someone is not just a strong feeling—it is a decision, it is a judgment, it is a promise" (Erich Fromm, *The Art of Loving*).

We learn to stake everything on another person, and we learn that it is worth it.

~Address, Prayer Vigil, Philadelphia,
September 26, 2015

Reflection: When people get married, they make vows. Even in nonreligious ceremonies where the couple makes up their own vows, the vows are traditionally accompanied by a wedding band or some other external symbol of their union. The wedding band is a sign that their love is not simply a feeling—it is also a fact.

As Catholics we are blessed with the knowledge that marriage is also a sacrament: it is a pledge to love Christ through another person, with the conviction that God's grace passes through the sacrament and makes it possible to stake so much on another human being.

Our families are founded on this certainty: that Christ is at the center, and he holds them together in hope. Lord, let us hope in you!

May 6

Learning to Give and Take
with Extraordinary Parents

CR

BY THE GRACE OF GOD children in grave difficulty are often given extraordinary parents, ready and willing to make every sacrifice. But these parents should not be left alone! We should accompany them in their toil, and also offer them moments of shared joy and lighthearted cheer.

~General Audience, April 8, 2015

Reflection: It is a beautiful thing to see parents care for children who are very sick! If we help support families who have great difficulties, it relieves them of their burden, but it also gives *us* a chance to watch grace in action.

There is so much for us to watch and to learn from families who struggle lovingly and patiently against the odds. Like mercy, it is an experience that blesses both him who gives and him who takes.

May 7

What the Angels Tell the Lord

CR

THE LORD JUDGES OUR LIFE according to what the angels of children tell him, angels who "always behold the face of the Father who is in heaven" (cf. Mt 18:10). Let us always ask ourselves: What will the children's guardian angels tell God about us?

~General Audience, April 8, 2015

Reflection: If you have to meet someone important or give a speech in front of famous people, you will usually practice what you're going to say beforehand. But not many people practice what they will say to children: most of what people say to kids comes out spontaneously.

What does the way we act without thinking say about us? Can we look at ourselves honestly and think what report the angels will give to God? If it's a bad report, we don't need to despair. But we can only change if we admit our shortcomings.

May 8

Happy in Our Problems and Our Work

ᛨ

MOTHERS, READY TO SACRIFICE SO MUCH FOR THEIR CHILDREN and often for others as well, ought to be listened to more. We should understand more about their daily struggle to be efficient at work and attentive and affectionate in the family.... A mother, with her children, always has problems, always work.

I remember there were five of us children at home, and while one was doing one thing, the other wanted to do another, and our poor mama went back and forth from one's side to another, but she was happy. She gave us so much.

~General Audience, January 7, 2015

Reflection: Mothers—whether they work outside the home or not—can often feel conflicted in the tasks they need to do. There is always so much—and it can be hard to prioritize well when there is *too* much. Mothers and non-mothers alike can think there is a secret to figuring out how to be more efficient so that everything gets done.

But the real secret is in giving ourselves to all that we do, even if it *doesn't* all get done, and trusting the Lord to see to the rest. Like the pope's mother, we can do much happily if we embrace all that we do and stop worrying about getting everything done.

May 9

Marrying in the Lord Is a Gift to All

ભ

WHEN CHRISTIANS MARRY "IN THE LORD," they are transformed into an effective sign of God's love. Christians do not marry for themselves alone: they marry in the Lord for the good of the entire community, society as a whole.

~General Audience, April 29, 2015

Reflection: Heaven has often been compared to a great wedding feast: a wedding is a celebration for the couple getting married, but it is also a party for everyone because God's love is manifested through the married couple—and more of God's love is always better!

Both in times of gladness *and* difficulty it is worth remembering that God's love can work through us, even if we don't always understand how.

May 10

Serving the Little Ones

ca

WHEN WE SEEK ABOVE ALL to prefer serving the little one, the out-cast, the sick, those who are overlooked and unloved … when we serve these little ones, we serve Jesus in the best way possible.

~Address, Vespers, Havana, Cuba, September 20, 2015

Reflection: In many fairy tales there is an ugly or tiny creature that ends up being wonderful and powerful by the end of the story. There is something powerful in serving the small, forgotten, and unloved. It transforms us, and them.

Let us always remember that Jesus himself became a tiny child in Bethlehem, a refugee in Egypt, a criminal hanged on a cross.

May 11

Do You Mind?

☙

BEFORE DOING ANYTHING IN YOUR FAMILY, ask: "Do you mind if I do this? Would you like me to do this?" This way of asking is well-mannered indeed, but it is also full of love. This does so much good for families.

~General Audience, May 13, 2015

Reflection: I have a good friend who loved carrot cake. For a long time, she wanted it every year for her birthday, but then she got sick of it. Thing is, her best friend still gets her a carrot cake every year on her birthday.

When we know people well, we naturally think we know them well enough to know what they want—or don't want. But we often don't.

Recognizing that the people I know still remain a mystery to me helps me love them better. Asking them what they'd like—instead of assuming we already know—shows them we're open to knowing them better and loving them more.

May 12

There Are No Perfect Families

Cℛ

NO DOUBT ABOUT IT: the perfect family does not exist; there are no perfect husbands and wives, perfect parents, perfect children....

Those families don't exist. But that does not prevent families from being the answer for the future. God inspires us to love, and love always engages with the persons it loves....

So let us care for our families, true schools for the future.

Let us care for our families, true spaces of freedom.

Let us care for families, true centers of humanity.

~Address, Meeting with Families,
Santiago, Cuba, September 22, 2015

Reflection: Jesus was God and therefore perfect. Mary was without original sin: pretty close! And St. Joseph was an extraordinarily holy man: a great saint. Despite all this, we don't call Jesus, Mary, and Joseph the Perfect Family. We call them the *Holy* Family.

They remind us that we are seeking what they did: true holiness, which we learn by keeping Christ at the center, just as they did.

May 13

How We Pray for Peace

CR

DEAR YOUNG PEOPLE, I ASK YOU to join me in praying for peace. You can do this by offering your daily efforts and struggles to God; in this way your prayer will become particularly precious and effective.
~Address, Meeting with Refugees and Disabled Children,
Pilgrimage to the Holy Land, May 24, 2014

Reflection: If you have worked with computers, you know how important it is to hit "save" while you're working on something. It's just one small action, one little button, but it makes all the difference. Otherwise, you can spend hours working on something and have it disappear.

God saves our action in the same way: we can work on things for years without success (or what we think is success). But praying redeems our efforts; it gives our everything over to him and entrusts it to his hands. This way, nothing is lost, and things that seem like impossible dreams—like peace—can become realities.

May 14

Mary: Truly a Mother

☙

MARY IS ATTENTIVE ... she is not closed in on herself, worried only about her little world. Her love makes her "outgoing" towards others.... Mary, quite simply, is a mother! She is there, attentive and concerned.

It is gratifying to hear this: Mary is a mother! I invite you to repeat this with me: *Mary is a mother!* Once again: *Mary is a mother!* And once more: *Mary is a mother!*

~Homily, Mass for Families,
Guayaquil, Ecuador, July 6, 2015

Reflection: When a woman becomes a mother, her whole life changes, because even when she thinks about herself, she thinks about another person. A mother may even think of her child's needs as her own. When Mary conceived Jesus that happened to her, too—and has never changed.

Whatever limits we and our own mothers may have, Mary is always there to mother us. Our needs are her needs, and she wants to help us with them.

May 15

Forgiveness Is for Our Sins, Too

CR

IF WE ARE NOT ABLE TO FORGIVE OURSELVES, then we are no longer able to forgive period.

~General Audience, May 13, 2015

Reflection: As Catholics, we have been given a great grace in sacramental confession. We have the opportunity to go someplace—a real place, with a real person!—and be forgiven by God. If he has forgiven us, who are we to disagree? We can always start again. Let us trust the Lord and take him at his word.

Lord, help me to be truly sorry for my sins, and fully capable of receiving your merciful forgiveness.

May 16

A Humble Home

CR

IT IS IMPORTANT THAT THE CHURCH IN THE UNITED STATES ... be a humble home, a family fire which attracts men and women through the attractive light and warmth of love....

We know well how much darkness and cold there is in this world; we know the loneliness and the neglect experienced by many people, even amid great resources of communication and material wealth. We also know their fear in the face of life, their despair, and the many forms of escapism to which it gives rise.

Consequently, only a Church which can gather around the family fire remains able to attract others. And not any fire, but the one which blazed forth on Easter morn.

~Address, Meeting with Bishops,
Washington, D.C., September 23, 2015

Reflection: Campfires are always a sign of human presence. Animals may love or fear fire, but only people know how to build fires. A burning fire brings warmth and light (and, sometimes, cooked food): it is a simple but powerful sign of presence.

Christ said that he came to cast fire on the earth, but that he wished it were already burning. Will we bring that blaze to the world?

May 17

Family: Home, Hospital, and School

☙

THE FAMILY IS THE NEAREST HOSPITAL; when a family member is ill, it is in the home that they are cared for as long as possible. The family is the first school for the young, the best home for the elderly.

~Homily, Mass for Families,
Guayaquil, Ecuador, July 6, 2015

Reflection: Anyone who has been sick in the hospital will tell you how important it is to have good nurses. It's so important to feel cared for! Our families—whether we live with them or not—give us the chance to be cared for, old or young. We never grow out of that need.

Lord, show me how to serve you in my family—with care and gladness.

May 18

His Joy and His Peace

☙

CHRISTIAN JOY IS A GIFT OF THE HOLY SPIRIT.... [But] where is this joy in the saddest moments, in times of anguish? Let's think about Jesus on the cross: Did he have joy? Eh, no! But, yes, he had peace!... Joy, in the moment of anguish, of trial, becomes peace.

~Homily, *Domus Sanctae Marthae*, May 15, 2015

Reflection: We live in a world of people who want to be happy. Of course, we all do! Christian joy is a great thing, and a powerful one: so powerful that suffering and death will not stop it.

In moments of suffering, joy doesn't look like a great big smiley face, but it brings a calm that otherwise would be impossible. The trick is to realize that joy can—and does—go along with suffering, and that it is a great gift: one that God longs to give to us.

Lord, give us your joy. And help us learn to ask for it.

May 19

The Beauty of Sport, the Beauty of Life

ఠ

IT IS BEAUTIFUL AND SIGNIFICANT that children and adults find in sports training and in participating in … competitions an incentive to live their life to the fullest. It is surely a challenge…. I encourage you to remain committed to helping one another discover your potential and to love life, to appreciate it with all its limitations and especially in all its beauty.

Never forget beauty: the beauty of life, the beauty of sport[s], that beauty which God has given us.

~Address, Special Olympic Athletes,
Rome, July 19, 2015

Reflection: Watching a really gifted athlete in motion is a beautiful thing. That's not usually the word we use, but it's true: A great athlete moves in an amazing and wonderful way, and it's beautiful to watch.

Training for sports is also challenging, and we can see in this fact a deeper truth: that whether we're talented athletes or not, we are all called to discover the beauty of all we've been given—and discovering that beauty will also be a challenge.

May 20

The Path of Hope

☙

MEETING A YOUNG PERSON WITHOUT HOPE IS ... like meeting a young retiree. There are young people who seem to have retired at the age of twenty-two. They are young people filled with existential dreariness, young people who have surrendered to defeatism, young people who whine and run away from life.

The path of hope is not an easy one. And it can't be taken alone. There is an African proverb which says, "If you want to go quickly, walk alone, but if you want to go far, walk with another."

~Address to Students, Havana, Cuba,
September 20, 2015

Reflection: Life is long, even if it's too short: we can get discouraged or confused easily. We need guidance, we need signposts, trail markers—and, most of all, we need someone to push us and inspire us when we are tired.

This isn't a big problem, unless we insist on going it alone, because then we only have our own strengths and energy to depend on. Let's not let our pride get in the way of our hope—the path of hope is the road less traveled, but it's very well marked.

May 21

Whose Team Are We On?

CR

St. Ignatius has a famous meditation on the two standards. He describes the standard of the devil and then the standard of Christ. It would be like the football jerseys of two different teams. And he asks us which team we want to play for....

St. Ignatius says that the devil, in order to recruit players, promises that those who play on his side will receive riches, honor, glory, and power. They will be famous. Everyone will worship them.

Then, Ignatius tells us the way Jesus plays. His game is not something fantastic. Jesus doesn't tell us that we will be stars, celebrities, in this life. Instead, he tells us that playing with him is about humility, love, service to others. Jesus does not lie to us; he takes us seriously.

~Address, Meeting with Young People,
Asunción, Paraguay, July 12, 2015

Reflection: Satan loves to make us think of things that aren't true, just like in the Garden of Eden, where he tricked Adam and Eve into believing they would becomes "like gods" but instead found death and suffering. He makes us think that by following him we will become powerful and happy. You may become powerful in the eyes of the world (or not), but you won't become happy. Why? Because the devil didn't make us—God did. He made us for himself, and so the devil's way won't bring us to happiness *or* bring us to heaven.

Jesus' honest approach seems hard, and it is in many ways. But it brings so much gladness to the people who follow it. People who play dirty sometimes win. But we don't call them winners.

Lord, help me see what truly winning is all about!

May 22

Understanding Our Place in Creation

CR

WE ARE NOT GOD. The earth was here before us and it has been given to us.

~*Laudato Si'*, 67

Reflection: The beginning of the Book of Genesis makes it clear that God intends the world for the use of humanity. It is also clear that the world is very, very good, and God loves it.

People who own a house—especially one that belonged to their parents before them—care for the house. They try to fix things when they're broken, they try to keep the floors in good condition, they clean it.

We are called to do even more with the earth, since it's more precious, longer lasting, and a clearer sign of God.

May 23

A Grandparent's Mission in Words

❧

HOW BEAUTIFUL ... IS THE ENCOURAGEMENT an elderly person manages to pass on to a young person who is seeking the meaning of faith and of life! It is truly the mission of grandparents, the vocation of the elderly. The words of grandparents have special value for the young. And the young know it.

I still carry with me, always, in my breviary, the words my grandmother consigned to me in writing on the day of my priestly ordination. I read them often, and they do me good.

~General Audience, March 11, 2015

Reflection: It is a great and beautiful witness when young people see someone who has lived a full life, who has suffered and experienced a lot, and who takes an interest in them and advises them. Even a few words—said out loud or written in a note—can make a huge difference in a young person's life.

May 24

Curing Discouragement

☙

I ENCOURAGE YOU TO BE ... FRIENDS TO THE POOR, and to make them feel that they are important in the eyes of God. May the difficulties that you surely meet not discourage you.

~Address, Meeting with the Food Bank
Foundation, Rome, October 3, 2015

Reflection: One of the most moving musical recordings I've ever heard was a homeless man singing the song "Jesus' Blood Never Failed Me Yet." It moved me for many reasons, but in particular, I thought, "If this homeless man can be certain of Jesus' sacrifice and love, and his goodness to him, why can't I?"

Sometimes we feel like complaining, until we realize we're talking to someone whose life is much more difficult than our own. Being friends to the poor is a great gift to ourselves: people who know they are poor often have a richer understanding of what is important and worthwhile. Are we ready to learn this?

May 25

No Place for Apathy

CR

WE DON'T WANT APATHY TO GUIDE OUR LIVES ... or do we? We don't want the force of habit to rule our life ... or do we? So we ought to ask ourselves: What can we do to keep our heart from growing numb, becoming anesthetized? How do we make the joy of the Gospel increase and take deeper root in our lives? Jesus gives the answer. He said to his disciples then, and he says it to us now: Go forth! Proclaim! The joy of the Gospel is something to be experienced, something to be known and lived only through giving it away, through giving ourselves away.

~Homily, Canonization Mass of Junípero Serra,
Washington, D.C., September 23, 2015

Reflection: Nike's "Just Do It" advertising campaign has had enduring appeal. Many of us think about doing something, but then we consider how little time, energy, and gear we have ... and go back to thinking about it. We get trapped in a cycle of boredom or uncertainty. But if we just get outside and run or play, we discover the excitement of doing something.

This happens with exercise, but also with our experience of Christianity. When we go out and proclaim Christ, when we share his good news and ourselves, we see him through new eyes, and we can't be bored anymore!

May 26

The Golden Rule

ର

"Do unto others as you would have them do unto you" (Mt 7:12). This rule points us in a clear direction. Let us treat others with the same passion and compassion with which we want to be treated. Let us seek for others the same possibilities which we seek for ourselves.

Let us help others to grow, as we would like to be helped ourselves.... The Golden Rule also reminds us of our responsibility to protect and defend human life at every stage of its development.

~Address, Visit to Joint Session
of U.S. Congress, September 24, 2015

Reflection: "Do unto others as you would have them do unto you"—the Golden Rule is part of Christ's teaching that is also common to other faith traditions. It is a starting point for a way of life that builds common ground in our culture. Treating others as we would like to be treated gives us a clear direction and measure.

It also helps us reflect on how we would most like to be treated: with kindness and patience, of course, but we also want to be protected and cared for, to grow and learn.

May 27

Let Him Surprise Us

CR

LET US ALLOW GOD TO SURPRISE US. He never tires of casting open the doors of his heart and of repeating that he loves us and wants to share his love with us.

~*Misericordiae Vultus*, Bull of Indiction
for the Year of Mercy, 25

Reflection: Many young children (and some older ones as well) close their eyes when a scary part happens in a movie; they may even cover their eyes with their hands to block out the scene. Sometimes, God lets us go through very difficult times that can be confusing and painful. When that happens, we are tempted to shut our eyes on life in order to block out the fear and pain—it's a natural instinct. We try not to look too hard.

But God is always looking to surprise us with his love, if we can just open our eyes to him.

Lord, open my eyes to seeing you!

May 28

Pressing Forward with Courage

∽

THE LORD ... ALWAYS TAKES US BY THE HAND lest we drown in the sea of our fears and anxieties. He is ever at our side; he never abandons us.

And so, let us not be overwhelmed by fear or disheartened, but with courage and confidence let us press forward in our journey and in our mission.

~Address, Meeting with Priests, Religious, Seminarians,
Mount of Olives, Jerusalem, May 26, 2014

Reflection: The ocean, the sea is very beautiful. But it can also be terrifying, as those who have experienced hurricanes and tsunamis know too well. It's natural to be afraid of it—and yet, Jesus was able to calm the sea.

Fear and anxieties are natural, too—we don't need to worry if we are afraid. But the Lord never abandons us, and he is always greater than anything that scares us. We have good reason for courage and confidence.

Lord, give me more courage and confidence in your greatness!

May 29

Our Greatest Good

CR

THE GREATEST GOOD WE CAN HAVE IN LIFE is our relationship with God. Are you convinced of this? Do you realize how much you are worth in the eyes of God? Do you know that you are loved and welcomed by him unconditionally, as indeed you are?

~Message for the Thirtieth World Youth Day, 2015

Reflection: Why is our relationship with God the greatest good in our lives? First of all, because he is always with us. He is the one thing we can never lose. But that alone isn't enough. It's also because his love for us is complete, unconditional, and the most satisfying thing there is. It's what we were made for.

Do I dare to believe this? How can I become more convinced of it?

May 30

The Great Gift of Faithful Families

CR

EVERY DAY, ALL OVER THE WORLD, the Church can rejoice in the Lord's gift of so many families who, even amid difficult trials, remain faithful to their promises and keep the faith!

~Address, Meeting with Bishops,
Philadelphia, September 27, 2015

Reflection: "Well done, good and faithful servant," the master says in the parable of the talents to the servant who invested wisely (see Mt 25). This is what the Lord says to families who keep their promises of the faith. He knows our trials, and rejoices in our faithfulness in spite of them.

The Lord is looking to entrust us with more and greater gifts. Can he count on us?

May 31

Mary Comes in Haste

Feast of the Visitation of the Blessed Virgin Mary

CR

[MARY WAS] A YOUNG WOMAN of perhaps between fifteen and seventeen years of age who, in a small village of Palestine, was visited by the Lord, who told her that she was to be the mother of the Savior. Mary was far from "thinking it was all about her," or thinking that everyone had to come and wait upon her; she left her house and went out to serve. First she goes to help her cousin Elizabeth....

The Gospel tells us that Mary went in haste, slowly but surely, with a steady pace, neither too fast nor so slow as never to get there. Neither anxious nor distracted, Mary goes with haste to accompany her cousin who conceived in her old age.

Henceforth this was always to be her way. She has always been the woman who visits men and women, children, the elderly and the young.

~ Homily, Mass, Santiago, Cuba, September 22, 2015

Reflection: It's always exciting for a city when a home team wins the World Series or the Super Bowl or the Stanley Cup. The parades that happen afterward are like an explosion of shared enthusiasm—when something good happens to us, we love to share our news with someone who appreciates how excited we are, and it's even better when our news is their news, too.

When the angel came to Mary, he didn't say much. He told her she would conceive and bear a son through the power of the Holy Spirit ... and he also told her that her cousin Elizabeth was pregnant through divine means.

Mary was a loving woman, and she went to Elizabeth to help her out. But she was excited to go, too. Here was her cousin, someone she could talk to about all the amazing things that had happened to both of them!

Mary wants to visit with us in the same way. She is looking forward to being with us. She comes in haste to us when we call her.

June 1

The Peace and Joy of Infinite Love

ೞ

IF WE OPEN THE DOOR TO JESUS and allow him to be part of our lives, if we share our joys and sorrows with him, then we will experience the peace and joy that only God, who is infinite love, can give.

~Message of Pope Francis for
Twenty-Ninth World Youth Day, 2014

Reflection: Life has its own moments of pleasure and joy. They can be wonderful, but are often short-lived. But God is infinite, and so he can give us infinite peace and joy if we open the door to him. He knocks—do we answer?

June 2

Taking Jesus Seriously

CR

JESUS CHALLENGES US, YOUNG FRIENDS, to take seriously his approach to life and to decide which path is right for us and leads to true joy. This is the great challenge of faith.... If you ... are able to say "yes" to Jesus, your lives will become both meaningful and fruitful.

~Message of Pope Francis for
Twenty-Ninth World Youth Day, 2014

Reflection: People have varied talents and abilities; some people are capable of things that others only dream of. We often think that being meaningful and fruitful depends on how talented and able we are.

But God made us all. He made us with different kinds of talents, and allows life circumstances that sometimes take away those abilities in unexpected ways, such as through disease, accidents, or war. But he then makes life meaningful and fruitful through circumstances that seem impossible.

This is part of our challenge—to say yes to him, trusting that he will make life worthwhile.

June 3

It Begins with Me

CR

SOME PEOPLE ONCE ASKED MOTHER TERESA of Calcutta what needed to change in the Church.... They asked her, where is the starting point? And she replied, you and I are the starting point!...

I make her words my own, and I say to you: Shall we begin? Where? With you and me!... Each one of you, open [your] heart, so that Jesus may tell you where to start.

~Address, Prayer Vigil, Rio de Janeiro,
Brazil, July 27, 2013

Reflection: It's easy to say what has to change ... in *other* people and institutions. But I also need to change! We all need conversion—that's why Jesus said he came for the sick, not those who are already well. This doesn't make us bad; it makes us human.

If we open our hearts to Christ, asking him to change us, we are already halfway there. He will never ignore you when you ask him to convert your heart!

June 4

The Spirit Lets Us Communicate to the World

CR

As on [the] day of Pentecost, the Holy Spirit is poured out constantly even today on the Church and on each one of us so we may … communicate to the entire world the merciful love of the Lord.

Communicating the merciful love of the Lord: this is our mission!

~*Regina Caeli*, May 24, 2015

Reflection: On the day of Pentecost, the people watching the apostles were amazed because they each heard the Gospel being spoken in their own language—they were from all over the world and spoke many different languages, but they understood these men who had never taken a single class in their language!

God didn't grant the *listeners* the ability to understand the apostles' language—he made the *apostles* capable of speaking new languages, which is a lot harder!

This is what the Holy Spirit does for us, if we call on him: He makes us able to communicate his love to the world in ways everyone can understand. This is our mission—let's ask him to complete it!

June 5

Immerse Yourselves in the Reality of Life

 CR

DEAR YOUNG PEOPLE, please, don't be observers of life ... get involved. Jesus did not remain an observer, but he immersed himself. Don't be observers, but immerse yourself in the reality of life, as Jesus did.

~Address, Prayer Vigil, Rio de Janeiro,
Brazil, July 27, 2013

Reflection: I don't have a very good sense of direction. For many years before I started driving, people would take me places, but I had no idea how we got there. I often looked out the window, but I didn't learn anything.

Once I started driving, though, I gained a better sense of where things were. It is good to observe, but there is a big difference between watching to learn and passive observation. Life is a great adventure. We need to prepare ourselves to enter it decisively!

June 6

Getting Enthusiasm from the Source

ဢ

ENTHUSIASM IS CONTAGIOUS. But do you know where this word comes from: *enthusiasm*? It comes from Greek, and it means, "to have something of God inside" or "to be inside God." Enthusiasm, when it is healthy, demonstrates this: that one has something of God inside and expresses him joyously.

~Address, Meeting with Young People,
Castelpetroso, Italy, July 5, 2014

Reflection: We all know the difference between morning people and night people. Some people struggle to get up early, while others struggle to stay awake at night. Our natural enthusiasm depends even on the time of day!

One of the beautiful things about being a Christian is that we have a source of enthusiasm that is greater than we are. When we don't know where to find enthusiasm for the tasks we have before us, we can ask him to reinvigorate us. He can give us the joy that is found in him (though we'll need to cooperate if we want to get all the sleep we need!)

June 7

Building a Great Life

CR

BUILD GREAT AND LASTING THINGS IN YOUR LIFE!... Do not content yourselves with little goals. Aspire to happiness, have courage, the courage to go outside of yourselves and bet on the fullness of your future together with Jesus.

~Address, Meeting with Young People,
Castelpetroso, Italy, July 5, 2014

Reflection: Sometimes people are criticized for straining the gnat and swallowing the camel (see Mt 23:24). The expression refers to people who make a big deal about minor details and then let big things slide. (My mother often used the expression in explaining how my father chose his ties.)

The biggest reason not to obsess over little details is because we cannot possibly pay attention to every little thing; when we start focusing on little goals, we let big and important things slip away. Can I step back and keep the big picture in mind?

June 8

Jesus Still Walks Our Streets

CR

KNOWING THAT JESUS STILL WALKS OUR STREETS, that he is part of the lives of his people, that he is involved with us in one vast history of salvation, fills us with hope. A hope which liberates us from the forces pushing us to isolation and lack of concern for the lives of others....

A hope which frees us from empty "connections"....

A hope which is unafraid of involvement....

A hope which makes us see, even in the midst of smog, the presence of God as he continues to walk the streets of our city. Because God is in the city.

~Homily, Mass, Madison Square Garden,
New York City, September 25, 2015

Reflection: Many of us—especially people who have lived in big cities—know the experience of being surrounded by people but feeling totally alone. But many also know the great energy and excitement that being around a lot of people can bring.

God continues to walk among us, but we can use our crowded cities and our crowded lives to distract us from him, or to look more carefully. Which will it be?

June 9

It's Impossible Alone

❧

WE CANNOT DO IT ALONE. In facing the pressure of events and trends, we will never manage to find the right path alone, and should we find it, we would not have enough strength to persevere, to face the climb and the unexpected obstacles.

And this is where the Lord Jesus' invitation comes in: "If you would ... follow me."

~Address, Meeting with Young People,
Castelpetroso, Italy, July 5, 2014

Reflection: The modern world encourages people to be independent and strong. We often look down on needy people. But the truth is that we cannot live alone—and we don't have to! If we are strong, he gave us our strength. When we are weak, he wants to sustain us.

In every circumstance, he is inviting us to follow him.

June 10

Unlimited Gift of the Spirit

ભ

POINTEDLY, YET AFFECTIONATELY, Jesus tells us: "If you, who are evil, know how to give good gifts to your children, how much more will the heavenly Father give the Holy Spirit to those who ask him!" (Lk 11:13). How much wisdom there is in these few words!

It is true that as far as goodness and purity of heart are concerned, we human beings don't have much to show! But Jesus knows that, where children are concerned, we are capable of boundless generosity. So he reassures us: if only we have faith, the Father will give us his Spirit.

~Homily, Closing Mass, World Meeting of Families,
Philadelphia, September 27, 2015

Reflection: It's pretty amazing how much people do for their children (even if kids don't always think so!), and it's especially striking with newborns. First-time parents may recall how, only recently, they were sleeping late and spending their free time entertaining themselves, while now they spend that same "free time" waking up to feed someone else and entertaining *her*!

It is a wonderful reminder of how much the presence of someone we love can change us.

Let's pray for the Holy Spirit to come into our lives with the same dedication with which we beg for a few more winks of sleep.

June 11

A Different Sort of Power

CR

POWER IS ... FLEETING, here today, gone tomorrow.... It's important if you can do good with power. Jesus defined power: true power is service, serving others, serving the poor.

~In-flight Press Conference,
September 27, 2015

Reflection: What is it, exactly, that we want with power? Do we want other people to do what we want? What do we really want?

When we realize that what we want is God himself, we start to understand power in a different way; suddenly, serving makes sense. Then we discover tremendous power, because it's God's infinite power that works through us.

When we stop being power-hungry, and serve him, we become truly powerful.

June 12

Go Out and Tell the Good News to Everyone

CR

JESUS DID NOT PROVIDE A SHORT LIST of who is, or is not, worthy of receiving his message and his presence. Instead, he always embraced life as he saw it. In faces of pain, hunger, sickness, and sin. In faces of wounds, of thirst, of weariness, doubt, and pity.

Far from expecting a pretty life, smartly dressed and neatly groomed, he embraced life as he found it. It made no difference whether it was dirty, unkempt, broken. Jesus said: Go out and tell the good news to everyone.

~Homily, Canonization Mass of Junípero Serra,
Washington, D.C., September 23, 2015

Reflection: An old advertising adage claims that "the medium is the message"—that how we say something *is* what we say. We all have natural preferences for certain kinds of people and certain ways of doing things. We want the glory of the Lord to look like our idea of it.

God has tried to break us of this from the beginning of his Incarnation: coming to a young unmarried woman and being born in a stable, the child of poor parents whose first visitors were poor shepherds. Nothing glamorous here.

This is his message: that there is no one—*no one*—unworthy of receiving him.

June 13

Why We Avoid Empty Homes

಄

IN MANY CULTURES TODAY ... we have fewer moments in common, to stay together, to stay at home as a family. As a result, we don't know how to be patient, we don't know how to ask permission, we don't know how to beg forgiveness, we don't know how to say "thank you," because our homes are growing empty. Not of people, but empty of relationships, empty of human contact, empty of encounters, between parents, children, grandparents, grandchildren, and siblings.

~Address, Meeting with Families,
Santiago, Cuba, September 22, 2015

Reflection: Many of us look at the living conditions of recent immigrants or previous generations and think, "How many people slept in one room?!" And we feel very lucky to be better off.

But while we may be richer in economic terms, those others were probably better off in human relationships; they had nowhere to hide, and so they had to deal with things more than we do—and learned from it. But so often we don't feel like dealing with people and their problems, and so we avoid them. This is a real loss—for ourselves, first of all!

Lord, help us not to avoid each other, but to welcome the opportunities that come with close quarters. Sustain us when we feel like we simply cannot handle things.

June 14

Free Hearts

CR

"LORD JESUS, GIVE ME A HEART THAT IS FREE.... That I may not be a slave to a false freedom, which means doing what I want at every moment."

~Address, Meeting with Young People,
Asunción, Paraguay, July 12, 2015

Reflection: Everybody wants to feel free! Often we think that being free is about doing whatever we want, whenever we want. We think we'll find freedom in getting away from people we want to avoid or things that we "have to do" so that we can do things that are more fun.

But when we think that way, our hearts aren't really free, because inside we're always fighting whatever the day brings.

Can I try to live today with a free heart, accepting that life might not go the way I would choose, but it is the beautiful and challenging way that God is calling me? Can I try to teach my heart to trust him so that I can be truly free?

June 15

Gaze Upon the Lord

ℭℛ

LET US GAZE UPON THE LORD IN PRAYER, in the Eucharist, in confession, in our brothers and sisters, especially those who feel excluded or abandoned. May we learn to see them as Jesus sees us.

Let us share his tenderness and mercy with the sick, prisoners, the elderly, and families in difficulty. Again and again we are called to learn from Jesus, who always sees what is most authentic in every person, which is the image of his Father.

~Homily, Mass, Holguín,
Cuba, September 21, 2015

Reflection: God makes himself present in the sacraments in a tangible way; Christ also gave us the Church so that he could be present through the faces of his people who remain physically present to us.

Lord, teach us to seek your face in everyone we meet; show us the image of your Father as we go about our day.

June 16

Left Out

CR

HOW MANY ELDERLY PEOPLE feel left out of family celebrations, cast aside and longing each day for a little love, from their sons and daughters, their grandchildren, their great-grandchildren?

~Homily, Mass for Families,
Guayaquil, Ecuador, July 6, 2015

Reflection: We all know what it's like to feel left out. It hurts to feel like everyone else is having fun when we haven't been invited to the party. I know how I feel when I'm left out, but I don't always realize when I am leaving out someone myself.

Are there people in my life who may be feeling left out? They may be elderly people—or people my own age. How can I bring them God's love today by including them in my life and my activities?

June 17

New Life in All Situations

ᏨᏵ

THE GOSPEL TEACHES US that the Spirit of Jesus can bring new life to every human heart and can transform every situation, even the most apparently hopeless. Jesus can transform all situations!

This is the message which you are called to share with your contemporaries: at school, in the workplace, in your families, your universities, and your communities.

~Address, Meeting with Asian Youth,
Dangjin, South Korea, August 15, 2014

Reflection: Nothing is impossible with God. There is nothing that cannot be changed, transformed. We need to be convinced of this down to the core of our being, because it is true. Once we realize its truth, we start to see it in action in all the circumstances of our lives.

We are called to bring this truth to the world; first, by bearing witness to the new life within us and sharing it with everyone we can.

June 18

The Gift of Presence

೧

A FATHER [MUST] BE *PRESENT* IN THE FAMILY ... close to his wife [and] close to his children as they grow: when they play and when they strive, when they are carefree and when they are distressed, when they are talkative and when they are silent, when they are daring and when they are afraid, when they take a wrong step and when they find their path again.

~General Audience, February 4, 2015

Reflection: We know how hard it is for families when the father is absent. Usually, when we think of good fathers, we think of all they do for their family—which is very good.

But their presence alone is a great gift. They remind us of the presence of God the Father, whose presence is always active, even when silent.

Are we willing to give the gift of our presence?

June 19

Jesus' Bride

☙

JESUS WAS NOT A CONFIRMED BACHELOR, far from it! He took the Church as his bride, and made her a people of his own. He laid down his life for those he loved, so that his bride, the Church, could always know that he is God with us, his people, his family.

~Address, September 26, 2015

Reflection: A man who is a "confirmed bachelor" lives alone and has no desire to change his life. Jesus never married, but his whole life was spent in love and sacrifice for those he loved; his life was determined by his love for his friends.

What does it mean that the Church is Jesus' bride? It means that he loves her, that he is united to her, and that he gives his entire self, even his body, to her as we see in holy Communion. And because we are the Church, we Catholics form her mystical body, and he gives himself to us and through us.

Lord, help me see what it means to be your people; let me be glad to be united to you in sacrifice.

June 20

Art, Beauty, God

ᘓ

BEAUTY BRINGS US TO GOD.... He is beauty and he is truth.... All that is good, all that is true, and all that is beautiful brings us to God. Because God is good; God is beauty; God is truth.

~Address, Prayer Vigil, Philadelphia,
September 26, 2015

Reflection: If you go to very poor places of the world, you might think that people wouldn't have time to think of beauty. But many medieval cities were populated by mostly poor people, who built beautiful cathedrals. In India, too (a very poor country), first-time visitors to the country comment on the amazing, vibrant colors of people's clothes.

In a culture that values utility and efficiency, we often think of beauty as an extra: something you add when you have extra time—or as something bad because it's materialistic. But beauty is part of God's very self, part of what we're made for.

We don't think of goodness or truth as an extra: beauty isn't either! Beauty brings us to wonder, to amazement, to contemplation. Let us be grateful and encouraging to those who bring us more beauty: they bring us to a sense of wonder for our Creator. That wonder is essential to our lives. We need it, because we don't live on bread alone.

June 21

Happiness Cannot Be Bought

CR

YOU CANNOT PURCHASE HAPPINESS. Whenever you buy happiness, you soon realize that it has vanished: The happiness you buy does not last. Only the happiness of love is the kind that lasts.

~Address, Meeting with Asian Youth,
Dangjin, South Korea, August 15, 2014

Reflection: Why does God command us to worship him, not idols—why is this the starting point for the Ten Commandments? It's not because God can't handle sharing his glory with idols—it's because idols won't satisfy; they make us waste our lives. Idols tease and confuse us, making us think they will make us happy. However, once we taste their fruit, we know better.

Trouble is, we don't always pay attention. This happens with money very easily. Money buys us things we like, which do bring us various forms of pleasure. But all pleasures naturally diminish over time, and so we need more and more for less and less satisfaction. So we think it's just a question of quantity: if we just buy a little more or get a better paying job or, or …

We need to stop this cycle. Money never has, and never will, lead us to true happiness. Once we accept this, we become truly open to the enduring happiness love brings.

June 22

Love of Neighbor Shows Our Love of God

ॐ

THE PATH OF LOVE IS SIMPLE: love God and love your neighbor, your brother or sister, the one at your side, who needs love and so many other things.

"But Father, how do I know that I love God?" Only if you love your neighbor, if you do not hate your neighbor and do not harbor hatred in your heart, do you love God. This is the sure proof.

~Address, Meeting with Asian Youth,
Dangjin, South Korea, August 15, 2014

Reflection: Love. It is a beautiful word and a more beautiful reality. It makes us think of happy and glad things—and rightly so. But the extravagant love that we have received from God compels us to love the same way: to love our neighbors—all of them.

Jesus tells us to love our enemies and pray for those who persecute us. This is the love that is asked of us; it's the same love Jesus gave his life for—he wants us to learn it as well.

June 23

Jesus' Strong and Sacred Heart

CR

NEVER STOP ASKING THE SACRED HEART for the gentleness that ... is patient, bears all things, hopes all things, and endures all things (cf. 1 Cor 13:4-7). This is the gentleness of Jesus' gaze when he looked at Peter on the night of Holy Thursday (cf. Lk 22:61), or when he invited Thomas, the disbeliever, to place his hand on his pierced Heart (cf. Jn 20:27).

It is there, from that Heart, that you will learn the gentleness you need ... in order to face even the most difficult and hostile situations.

~Address to the Comboni Missionaries
of the Sacred Heart, Rome, October 1, 2015

Reflection: When we think of hearts, we think of love. Usually, easy love: the kind that comes quickly and naturally.

But if we think about our actual physical hearts, we recognize that while our heart is delicate in some ways, it is a workhorse: its job is to bring our blood throughout our bodies, bringing oxygen and nutrients to every part of our physical being. It also feels all the changes in our bodies, and responds to them.

This is what Jesus' Sacred Heart does: it brings his breath and life to all the parts of our soul; it helps us adapt more gently to difficult situations, even those that threaten to take our breath away.

Lord, make new hearts within us!

June 24

Comfort in Prayer

 CR

FIND COMFORT ... IN THE POWER OF PRAYER, in Jesus. Keep praying to him daily. He will not disappoint you. Jesus ... is the secret to keeping a joyful heart.

~Address, Meeting with Civic Leaders,
Asunción, Paraguay, July 11, 2015

Reflection: When we talk about the power of prayer, we usually think of how prayer changes things: a sick person gets better or we find a new job or a new friend—that is, we get the things we prayed for. This can be true, and it's wonderful.

But the greatest power of prayer is that it changes my heart. Prayer keeps my heart open and joyful even when life is hard and things *don't* seem to change. This is the key way in which Jesus doesn't disappoint: I don't always get what I asked for, but I always get him, and he changes my heart.

June 25

Go Forward!

CR

COURAGE! THIS IS A VIRTUE and an attribute of young people. The world needs courageous, not fearful, young people. It needs young people on the move, not standing still: there is no progress if the young stand still! Young people who are always motivated, not young people who retire! It's sad! It's sad to see a retired young person.

No, a young person should go forward on this road of courage. Go forward! This will be your victory; your job is to help change this world, to make it so much better.

~Address, Phone Call to Catholic Scouts,
Italy, August 10, 2014

Reflection: "Youth is wasted on the young," some people say. Why? Because it's hard to realize what great gifts you have when you're young: your energy, your enthusiasm, even your restlessness is a gift because it keeps you from being satisfied with small things.

But we live in a world that's very fearful, and so we need an extra dose of strength and courage, young and old alike. Courage doesn't mean we're free from fear. It means we don't let fear stop us. When we don't have that courage, we can always ask for it.

Lord, give me courage: fortify and strengthen me in you.

June 26

We Can't Grow by Avoiding Relationships

CR

WE DO NOT GROW IN THE LOVE OF GOD by avoiding the entanglement of human relations. For in loving others, we learn to love God, in stooping down to help our neighbor, we are lifted up to God.

~Homily, Vigil in Preparation for
Synod of Bishops, Rome, October 3, 2015

Reflection: Relationships, like politics, are messy. People are messy. But God, in his mysterious way, chose to enter the world and get involved in our messiness: he didn't send us a book, he didn't hit us with divine lightning, he didn't snap his fingers to save us—though he could have. Instead, he became a man, clearly showing us that we can't skip over human reality to get to him. That means dealing with other people, trying to understand and love them, in all their messy brokenness and in all of our own. Somehow, mysteriously, the Lord comes to us through these.

June 27

The Value of Wasting Time

ಞ

As bishop of Buenos Aires ... I often asked fathers if they played with their children, if they had the courage and love to spend time with their kids. And the answer was negative in most cases: "But I can't, because I have so much work ..."

And the father was absent from the little child growing up, he did not play with him, no, he did not waste time with him.

~General Audience, January 28, 2015

Reflection: Being present and being *truly* present is not the same thing. I can be "there" without paying attention or being interested in what someone is saying. In a world where we care so much about making our time productive, so many things can feel like a waste of time.

But when I give someone the gift of my attention and presence, it is a great thing. Let's not let the world trick us into believing that it's a waste of time!

June 28

Put It into Practice

ভ

LET ME GIVE YOU SOME ADVICE: the Gospel which you hear in the liturgy, read it again to yourself, in silence, and apply it to your life; and with Christ's love, received in holy Communion, you can put it into practice.

The Lord calls each one of you to work in his field; he calls you to be joyous leaders in his Church, ready to communicate to your friends what he has communicated to you, especially his mercy.

~Address to German Altar Servers,
Rome, August 5, 2014

Reflection: Sometimes, when we're tired, we may read something, and then if we read the same thing again, we don't realize we already read it! This can happen with many other things as well. Sometimes, we need to take extra time to go over something we didn't read or understand with full awareness the first time.

Reading the Gospel again on our own is a great practice, and with prayer and grace Christ will bring rich fruit from this simple thing. Can I spend a little extra time—even a couple of minutes—reading and meditating today?

June 29

Children Are Always a Gift

୧

CHILDREN ARE THE JOY OF THE FAMILY and of society.... Children are a gift, they are a gift: understood? Children are a gift. Each one is unique and irreplaceable; and at the same time unmistakably linked to his or her roots.

~General Audience, February 11, 2015

Reflection: When my brother was in elementary school and a child got very irritating in class, his teacher—who was a nun—would start responding to him by saying, "Yes, child of God." She did it to remind her that this child—however crazy he was making her—was a beloved child of God. He was a gift.

We are all children of God. We are all gifts, however crazy we sometimes make one another. Let's not forget!

June 30

Please and Thank You

ॐ

IN THE FAMILY WE LEARN how to ask without demanding, to say "thank you" as an expression of genuine gratitude for what we have been given, to control our aggressivity and greed, and to ask forgiveness when we have caused harm, when we quarrel, because in all families there are quarrels.

The challenge is to then ask for forgiveness. These simple gestures of heartfelt courtesy help to create a culture of shared life.

~Homily, Mass for Families,
Guayaquil, Ecuador, July 7, 2015

Reflection: So many times, saying please, thank you, and I'm sorry seem like small things—and even unimportant. How many times do we apologize without really meaning it? Or say thank you without actually being grateful? Don't we hate it when someone gives us a fake apology? These may be small things, but they're not unimportant.

The next time I apologize or say thank you, can I put my whole heart into what I'm saying and really try to mean it?

July 1

Gift of Youth

CR

YOU AND YOUR FRIENDS ARE FILLED with the optimism, energy, and good will which are so characteristic of this period of life. Let Christ turn your natural optimism into Christian hope, your energy into moral virtue, your good will into genuine self-sacrificing love!… In this way your youth will be a gift to Jesus and to the world.

~Homily, Sixth Asian Youth Day,
Haemi Castle, South Korea, August 17, 2014

Reflection: Young people tend to be more optimistic, while older people tend to be more cynical. Youthful optimism is a natural thing, but if I turn to Christ, he strengthens and deepens that natural optimism and makes it the foundation of genuine and lasting virtues.

Christ can take our fragile enthusiasms and give us a deep and abiding love for life and goodness. Who doesn't want that?

July 2

Family Formation

CR

FAMILIES ARE THE FIRST PLACE in which we are formed as persons and, at the same time, the "bricks" for the building up of society.

~Homily, Mass with Rite of Marriage,
St. Peter's Square, Rome, September 14, 2015

Reflection: From the beginning of creation, God wanted people to live in families. His essence is unity in three persons and he wants us, too, to be united despite our differences, and to learn to even love those differences.

We need our families in order to be ourselves: it is in our families that we learn who we are—but the world needs our families just as much as we do. Society is built through our families, one step at a time.

Family life involves many small details, but its mission is as vast as the world itself.

July 3

What We Learn at Home

CR

IT IS IN THE HOME THAT WE LEARN fraternity and solidarity, we learn not to be overbearing.

It is in the home that we learn to receive, to appreciate life as a blessing, and to realize that we need one another to move forward.

It is in the home that we experience forgiveness, and we are constantly invited to forgive and to grow.

It is interesting that in the home there is no room for "putting on masks": we are who we are, and in one way or another we are called to do our best for others.

~Address, Meeting with Families,
Santiago, Cuba, September 22, 2015

Reflection: If you don't see someone for a while, you can be amazed at how much she or he has changed. But if you're around someone frequently, it can take some time to notice. The same thing can happen in families. We are transformed by our lives together, but it's a process that may feel slow on the inside.

Family life gives us so many opportunities to practice patience, to give and receive apologies, to see the good in someone despite failings. We have so many opportunities to grow.

If we allow God to work in us, we are transformed by our everyday lives, even if it may take us a while to notice!

July 4

Staying True to Our Principles

CR

THE DECLARATION OF INDEPENDENCE stated that all men and women are created equal, that they are endowed by their Creator with certain inalienable rights, and that governments exist to protect and defend those rights....

We remember the great struggles which led to the abolition of slavery, the extension of voting rights, the growth of the labor movement, and the gradual effort to eliminate every kind of racism and prejudice directed at further waves of new Americans.

This shows that, when a country is determined to remain true to its principles, those founding principles based on respect for human dignity, it is strengthened and renewed.

~Address, Meeting for Religious Liberty,
Philadelphia, September 26, 2015

Reflection: A popular bumper sticker says, "Freedom isn't free." Those stickers remind people that political freedom also comes with a cost: there are soldiers who died in order to defend and protect the country and the freedom that Americans can easily take for granted.

But fighting for freedom isn't just for the military. Being true to the founding principles of the Declaration of Independence requires an ongoing commitment; it requires a willingness to sacrifice for the dignity of all, which is founded in our certainty that we are all God's children and that his love is for all of us.

July 5
Worth the Effort

ଔ

OUR HEARTS REJOICE when we see children grow up and make a home of their own. For a moment, we see that everything we worked for was worth the effort. To raise children, to support and encourage them, to help them want to make a life for themselves and form a family: this is a great challenge for parents.

~Address, Meeting with Families,
Santiago, Cuba, September 22, 2015

Reflection: A friend told me that for years she tried to get her kids to use their manners—to introduce themselves to people, say thank you, that sort of thing. She felt like she was beating a dead horse. But when they turned eighteen, suddenly they started doing all the things she had encouraged for years without success.

Parents (and children!) may have many moments where they feel like they've wasted their time. But then something happens—and it's like the sun breaking through the clouds. Jesus doesn't want us to waste our time.

When we can't see the fruit of our labors, let's turn to him in prayer so that he can show us the way. And when we see our children grown and starting out on their own, let us recognize the many gifts we have received!

July 6
Ask the Lord to Show You the Way

ത

DEAR YOUNG PEOPLE, some of you may not yet know what you will do with your lives. Ask the Lord, and he will show you the way. The young Samuel kept hearing the voice of the Lord who was calling him, but he did not understand or know what to say. Yet, with the help of the priest Eli, in the end he answered: Speak, Lord, for I am listening (cf. 1 Sm 3:1-10).

You, too, can ask the Lord: What do you want me to do? What path am I to follow?

~Address, Meeting with Volunteers, World Youth Day,
Rio de Janeiro, Brazil, July 27, 2013

Reflection: Sometimes we think God doesn't speak to us. We may think, "That's very nice for Samuel and King David and Moses and all, but that's not how my life goes."

Let's remember that even Samuel—who was called to be a prophet and lived with another prophet—didn't recognize God's voice or understand the Lord's call right away. He needed Eli to explain to him who was calling him. And then he had to be quiet in order to listen to the Lord.

We need wiser people, people we trust, to help guide us in recognizing the Lord, and then we need to be silent so that we can hear. But make no mistake, God speaks to us, too.

July 7

Jesus Likes Being Part of a Family

☙

JESUS BEGAN HIS LIFE WITHIN A FAMILY, within a home. And it is precisely our homes into which he continues to enter, and of which he becomes a part. He likes to be part of a family.

~Address, Meeting with Families,
Santiago, Cuba, September 22, 2015

Reflection: Jesus lived at home for many years before venturing on his public ministry. As a carpenter, he may even have worked at home. He wants to be part of our family lives as well—working, playing, eating. He's happy to join us for all of it.

July 8
Weary Slaves of Success

CR

WHEN WE LOOK ONLY FOR SUCCESS, pleasure, and possessions … we become enslaved, never satisfied, always looking for more. It is a tragic thing to see a young person who "has everything" but is weary and weak.

~Message of Pope Francis for
Twenty-ninth World Youth Day, 2014

Reflection: I have known many rich people, but very few rich people who thought they had enough. It's a funny thing: Many of us seek success in order to feel free, to be able to do what we want and buy what we want. But we get trapped very easily in looking for more.

We're right to think we need more—but it's a different *kind* of more. It's a difference in quality, not quantity. Are we willing to look honestly at our lives and ourselves? Do we have the courage to try a different tactic—or a different track—when we find ourselves weary and weak from our pursuit of pleasure and success?

July 9

His Boundless Love in Our Brothers and Sisters

֍

THE BOUNDLESS LOVE OF OUR FATHER ... comes to us, in Jesus, through our brothers and sisters. Faith teaches us to see that ... the light of God's face shines on me through the faces of my brothers and sisters.

~*Lumen Fidei,* June 29, 2013

Reflection: When we think of someone we love, and who loves us, our faces often change expression. Someone looking at us may even ask us, "What—or who—are you thinking about?"

God comes to us, today, through the faces of our brothers and sisters in Christ. Do I look for his light in them?

July 10

Letting Go of Anger

CR

AT TIMES HOW HARD IT SEEMS TO FORGIVE! And yet ... to let go of anger, wrath, violence, and revenge are necessary conditions to living joyfully. Let us therefore heed the apostle's exhortation: "Do not let the sun go down on your anger" (Eph 4:26).

~*Misericordiae Vultus*, Bull of Indiction for the Year of Mercy, 9

Reflection: When we are really angry, it seems impossible to forgive—because we believe we are *right* and have been wronged by someone! Many times, we *have* been wronged, and we *are* right.

But when we are angry, we lose perspective. We forget how many times the Lord has forgiven us. We lose sight of the good that the Lord wants for the other person. When we don't know how to forgive, can we at least pray for the desire to learn?

July 11

Joyful Christians

ॐ

CHRISTIANS ARE JOYFUL; THEY ARE NEVER GLOOMY. God is at our side. We have a Mother who always intercedes for the life of her children, for us.... Sin and death have been defeated....

If we are truly in love with Christ, and if we sense how much he loves us, our heart will "light up" with a joy that spreads to everyone around us.

~Homily, Shrine of Our Lady of Aparecida,
Brazil, July 24, 2013

Reflection: Christians are joyful, not gloomy, the pope tells us. This doesn't mean that Christians are always happy, that nothing bad happens to us, or that we don't suffer. It just means what the pope says next: that God is at our side and that we have a Mother who always intercedes for us.

Hard, bad things still happen to us. But it's different when those things happen and your all-powerful best friend is at your side. When our best friend is there, sometimes we even manage to laugh through our tears.

Lord, let my heart light up with your joy.

July 12

Family Perseverance

CR

THE PERSEVERANCE WHICH IS CALLED FOR in having a family and raising it transforms the world and human history. Families transform the world and history.

~Address, Meeting with Bishops,
Philadelphia, September 27, 2015

Reflection: Behind every famous person is a family who was there first and formed their personality. Many times, when children are young, they ask their parents to do something with them or for them, but their parents say they are too busy. Then, when the kids grow up, the situation reverses: it is the parents who are asking and the kids who say they are too busy.

Some of this is inevitable. Being a parent includes many responsibilities, and we all need to realize that we are not the center of the world and can't simply demand another person's attention.

But what are we busy with? When we love our families and spend time showing them our care and concern, we are transforming the world and history. When we're busy, let's make sure it's with things that really count.

July 13

There's No Diluting Our Faith in Jesus

☙

PLEASE DO NOT WATER DOWN YOUR FAITH in Jesus Christ. We dilute fruit drinks—orange, apple, or banana juice—but please do not drink a diluted form of faith. Faith is whole and entire, not something that you water down. It is faith in Jesus. It is faith in the Son of God made man, who loved me and who died for me.

~Address, Meeting with Young People
from Argentina, Rio de Janeiro, Brazil, July 25, 2013

Reflection: When we dilute a drink, we figure we're just making it easier to drink—not as strong, so the taste doesn't overwhelm us. But when you dilute something, you add something else (like water), and so you get something pretty different.

Our faith in Jesus is something strong: it may even be a little too strong for our taste, a little uncomfortable at times. But it is that very strength that makes it powerful. Let's not replace that power with something less, just because it's easier. We lose the best part that way.

July 14

Love Is Service

 C&

SERVICE IS THE SIGN OF TRUE LOVE. Those who love know how to serve others. We learn this especially in the family, where we become servants out of love for one another. In the heart of the family, no one is rejected; all have the same value.

~Homily, Mass for Families,
Guayaquil, Ecuador, July 6, 2015

Reflection: If we love someone, we're happy to help him or her. If we are passionate about a sport or an activity, we love doing it; we love showing others how we do it and how they can, too. It's service because it's useful for them, but it's useful for us, too, because it helps us remember our enthusiasm.

Things start to feel hard when we lose our love or the sense that our contribution is valued. Lord, help me to love so that I can serve happily!

July 15

Your Problems Are Mine

☙

IN A FAMILY, PARENTS, GRANDPARENTS, AND CHILDREN feel at home; no one is excluded. If someone has a problem, even a serious one, even if he brought it upon himself, the rest of the family comes to his assistance; they support him. His problems are theirs.

~Address, Meeting with Civic Leaders,
Quito, Ecuador, July 7, 2015

Reflection: There is a saying, "Many hands make light work," meaning if many people contribute to a task, it goes much faster and feels easier. If someone helps you with your chores, they go more quickly. When someone lends you a hand, you feel better because it makes life easier and because you remember that you're not alone.

Is there someone in your family who needs assistance? Is there someone you can help with a problem—or a burdensome task—today?

July 16

No Need to Fear

CR

JESUS, I PRAY FOR ALL THOSE YOUNG BOYS AND GIRLS who do not know that you are their strength and who are afraid to live, afraid to be happy, afraid to have dreams. Jesus, teach them how to dream, to dream big, to dream beautiful things, things which, although they seem ordinary, are things which enlarge the heart.

Lord Jesus, give us strength. Give us a free heart. Give us hope. Give us love and teach us how to serve. Amen.

~Address, Meeting with Young People,
Asunción, Paraguay, July 12, 2015

Reflection: "Once burned, twice cautious," the saying goes, and we often do feel the need to be cautious. Not only cautious in our actions, but cautious in our hopes as well. It's as if we didn't really believe anything truly extraordinary could be true.

But our God rose from the dead! With him, anything is possible. He wants to enlarge our hearts. Let us let him in by not being afraid to hope in him.

July 17

Appreciating the Help of Siblings

ଔ

WE SEE THE CARE, THE PATIENCE, THE AFFECTION that envelop *the weakest little brother or sister*, sick or physically challenged. There are countless brothers and sisters who do this, throughout the world, and perhaps we do not appreciate their generosity enough.

And when there are many siblings in a family ... the eldest boy or girl helps the dad, the mom, to take care of the younger children. This work of helping among siblings is beautiful.

~General Audience, February 18, 2015

Reflection: Most of us recognize the work that parents do in their families, but in many places in the world siblings do a lot of work for the family, too. Older siblings help care for younger ones; they help out in the home and in that way help both their parents and their brothers and sisters. They can also help the younger children learn.

The younger children, in turn, keep the older children playing and laughing even when they think they're too grown up. They let them have fun without feeling as embarrassed. This way of life together warms parents' hearts—and God's as well.

July 18

Why Complain?

CR

THERE IS ALWAYS THE OPTION OF COMPLAINING. But even complaint acts like a boomerang; it comes back and ends up increasing one's unhappiness.

~Address, Meeting with the Bishops of Brazil,
Rio de Janeiro, Brazil, July 28, 2013

Reflection: People sometimes say, when you ask how they are doing, "I can't complain." Of course, you *can* always complain—but is it useful?

The act of complaining reminds us of all that is difficult, everything that we dislike—and it engages our friends in thinking and talking about the same.

It's much better to cultivate gratitude, even if we don't see what there is to be grateful for at first; it gets easier as we work at it. Looking for things to be grateful for keeps our eyes fixed on what's bigger and better in our lives.

July 19

Caring for Our Home

CR

THE EARTH, OUR HOME, is beginning to look more and more like an immense pile of filth.

~Laudato Si', 21

Reflection: Little children don't always take care of their things, so you can't tell whether or not they like something by how they treat it. But as they grow up, they learn to take care of the things that matter to them.

If we care about things, but don't treat them well, it is a sign that we need to grow up in some important way. How is the Lord calling me to mature in the way I treat the world?

July 20

Our Elders Are Us

ଔ

OUR ELDERS ARE MEN AND WOMEN, fathers and mothers, who came before us on our own road, in our own house, in our daily battle for a worthy life. They are men and women from whom we have received so much.

The elder is not an alien. We are that elder: in the near or far future, but inevitably, even if we don't think it. And if we don't learn how to treat the elder better, that is how we will be treated.

~General Audience, March 4, 2015

Reflection: The commandment to honor your father and mother refers especially to taking care of parents when they are old. The Ten Commandments are a great gift to God's people, because they lay out a simple way of following God in both our hearts and our actions. They help us see the truth of our own selves.

If we see our parents as burdens, sooner or later that is how we will see ourselves—and perhaps how our children will see us. Caring for our parents—and for the elderly in general—is caring for the truth of ourselves and our God. Nothing less is at stake.

July 21

Training for Life

CR

JESUS ASKS US TO FOLLOW HIM FOR LIFE, he asks us to be his disciples, to "play on his team."... Now, what do players do when they are asked to join a team? They have to train, and to train a lot!

The same is true of our lives as the Lord's disciples.... Jesus offers us something bigger than the World Cup!... But he asks us to ... train ourselves, "to get in shape" so that we can face every situation in life undaunted, bearing witness to our faith....

Dear young people, be true "athletes of Christ!"

~Address, Prayer Vigil, World Youth Day,
Rio de Janeiro, Brazil, July 27, 2013

Reflection: Why do people—athletes, soldiers, others—train? It's so that their minds, hearts, and bodies can all be on the same page. Even if we think of ourselves as, say, training for speed, the speed is partially a consequence of all parts of ourselves being united in what we do: because they're more united, they can also work faster.

Christ wants us to train like this, too, so that our whole selves are united with him. Even training is fun if you love what you do—and why you do it! And there is nothing better than Jesus and being on his team.

July 22

Let Jesus Help You Up

ೞ

Speak to Jesus, and if you make a mistake in your life, if you should fall, if you should do something wrong, don't be afraid. [Say,] "Jesus, look at what I have done, what must I now do?"

Speak continually with Jesus, in the good times and in the bad, when you do right, and when you do wrong. Do not fear him!

~Address, Prayer Vigil, World Youth Day,
Rio de Janeiro, Brazil, July 27, 2013

Reflection: When children are small and fall down, they usually look up at their mothers. If their mothers don't look worried, many times they'll get right up and keep playing without crying. But if their mothers *do* look concerned, then they get nervous, too, and start to cry.

When you fall down, Jesus is waiting to look at you, just like a mother, and help you get right back up. He wants to help you get up, but you need to look at him. He looks back with a love even greater than a mother's!

July 23
On the Offensive

⚜

YOUNG PEOPLE, PLEASE, DON'T PUT YOURSELVES at the tail end of history. Be active members [of the Church]! Go on the offensive! Play down the field, build a better world, a world of brothers and sisters, a world of justice, of love, of peace, of fraternity, of solidarity. Play always on the offensive!

~Address, Prayer Vigil, World Youth Day,
Rio de Janeiro, Brazil, July 27, 2013

Reflection: "The best defense is a good offense," we often hear—because without an offensive strategy, you can't score. While defensive strategy is essential and important to any sport, it's not what wins the game.

Let's be faithful, true to our gifts, and go on the offensive in life as well, confident and glad to have the chance to reach our goal.

July 24

Stay Strong in Christ

ॐ

YOUNG PEOPLE WHO CHOOSE CHRIST *are* strong: they are fed by his word, and they do not need to "stuff themselves" with other things! Have the courage to swim against the tide. Have the courage to be truly happy!

Say no to [a] throwaway culture, a culture that assumes that you are incapable of taking on responsibility and facing the great challenges of life!

~Message of Pope Francis for
Twenty-ninth World Youth Day, 2014

Reflection: When people are dieting, they are usually told to go food shopping *after* they've eaten. In this way they won't be as tempted to buy junk food just because they're hungry. When we are fed by Christ's word, we are strengthened by him and aren't as tempted by the junk of our culture.

It feels good to be strong—and even better to see that strength in action. When we choose Christ, we find the strength to resist the uglier undercurrents in our world.

July 25
Think Big

☙

WE RISK SETTLING FOR LESS AND "THINKING SMALL" when it comes to the meaning of life. Think big instead! Open your hearts! As Blessed Pier Giorgio Frassati once said: "To live without faith, to have no heritage to uphold, to fail to struggle constantly to defend the truth: this is not living. It is scraping by. We should never just scrape by, but really live."

~Message of Pope Francis for
Twenty-ninth World Youth Day, 2014

Reflection: There's a song whose opening lines are "Life … is bigger." Life *is* big; and it is meant for something bigger still—who hasn't had that feeling in looking at the night sky?

When we live small, when we "scrape by," it's because we are trapped by our fears and keep our heads down instead of looking up. We have a great heritage to uphold: great and liberating truths to live by.

Lord, help me to look up!

July 26

An Amazing Grandma

Feast of St. Anne

CR

TODAY IS THE FEAST OF ST. ANNE, whom I like to call Jesus' grandma, and today is a beautiful day to celebrate grandmothers....

St. Anne is the woman who prepared her daughter to become queen, to become queen of heaven and earth. This woman did a good job!

~Homily, Mass, Caserta, Italy, July 26, 2014

Reflection: St. Anne did an amazing job! Like her daughter, she was called to a very special task: She became the mother of a daughter who was greater than herself; just as Mary was called to be mother to a Son even greater than herself.

Grandparents often step in for parents when mothers and fathers cannot fulfill all their responsibilities—what tremendous wisdom, faithfulness, and love they demonstrate. They can nurture in their grandchildren a sense of the greatness of God's world and the call of the Lord to serve in ways they might never have imagined or expected.

Let us give thanks for our grandparents today, for all they've done. And if they are still with us, let's tell them directly!

July 27

Always Children to Him

༼

CHILDREN REMIND US ... that we are always sons and daughters. Even if one becomes an adult, or an elder, even if one becomes a parent, if one occupies a position of responsibility, underneath all of this is still the identity of a child. We are all sons and daughters.

~General Audience, March 18, 2015

Reflection: We are all born children. Even when we grow up, we are still someone's child, and we are all, eternally, God's children. When children are small, they often try to show off their abilities to their parents, demonstrating the "amazing" things they can do.

Parents usually aren't impressed by the outcome, but they are impressed by the effort of the child, or the affection children show in what they do.

God always sees us like that. We don't need to impress him with our accomplishments, but we can impress him with the efforts of our love.

July 28

The Best Is Yet to Come

CR

FOR FAMILIES, THE RICHEST, DEEPEST, AND MOST BEAUTIFUL THINGS are yet to come.... The best wine will come to those who today feel hopelessly lost.

Say it to yourselves until you are convinced of it. Say it to yourselves, in your hearts: the best wine is yet to come. Whisper it to the hopeless and the loveless. Have patience, hope, and follow Mary's example—pray, open your heart, because the best wine is yet to come.

God always seeks out ... those who drink only of discouragement. Jesus feels their weakness, in order to pour out the best wines for those who, for whatever reason, feel that all their jars have been broken.

~Homily, Mass for Families,
Guayaquil, Ecuador, July 6, 2015

Reflection: Jesus' first miracle is at the wedding feast of Cana, and it is truly a sign of what is to come. He does what no one ever does (at least at weddings!): he saves the best for last.

It didn't make sense. Everyone was surprised by it. Everyone serves the best first. We expect this in our lives as well. We expect our enthusiasm to start strong and then die out. Because God's logic doesn't seem to make sense, sometimes we don't dare to believe it. But he has his own logic, and if we can learn to be patient and to trust, he will not disappoint us.

July 29

Important to Me

CR

JOY ... IS HEARING SOMEONE SAY, but not necessarily with words, "You are important to me." This is beautiful.... In calling you, God says to you, "You are important to me, I love you, I am counting on you."

Jesus says this to each one of us! Joy is born from that!

~Address, Meeting with Seminarians
and Novices, Rome, July 6, 2013

Reflection: People complain about feeling ignored—and, of course, it feels bad to be ignored. If you love people, you cannot ignore them (even sometimes when you want to!)—they are too important. When someone feels down, they may say they don't matter, and we may remind them, "You matter to *me*; you're important to *me*."

Knowing how important we are to *God*, how much he loves us and is counting on us—on us!—is the greatest source of joy.

Lord, let me know my own importance—and the importance of those around me.

July 30

The Strength of Forgiveness

CR

THERE IS A CONDITION FOR PRAYING WELL … we can pray well and say "Father" to God only if our heart is at peace with others, with our brothers and sisters….

To one who justifies herself saying: "this person did this to me, this one did this and that to me" … there is only one response: "forgive, forgive as he will forgive you!"…

Forgiveness is a great strength: One needs to be strong in order to forgive.

~Homily, *Domus Sanctae Marthae*, June 18, 2015

Reflection: We Christians call God our Father. He is Lord, but he is also *dad*. He is my Father, but he is also *our* Father. When Jesus taught us to pray, he instructed us to say "Our Father"—which means that I have siblings, too! I have brothers and sisters who share our home, even if I'm an only child.

Part of living in peace in my Father's home is living in peace with my brothers and sisters. Forgiving them—and asking God to help me forgive them when I don't know how. When I don't know how to pray, I can start there.

July 31

Approaching Jesus

༼ཙ

AM I CONCERNED ONLY WITH MY RELATIONSHIP WITH JESUS, [am I] closed [in], selfish?...

Do I distance people from Jesus?

Or do I ... hear the cry of so many people and help them to approach Jesus?

~Homily, *Domus Sanctae Marthae*, May 28, 2015

Reflection: When Jesus rose from the dead, the angels asked Mary Magdalen, "Whom do you seek?" This is the same question he asks us every day.

What are you really looking for? Whom do you seek? The answer I give to this question changes the way I approach everything, and whether I lead people to Jesus or away from him.

August 1

Radical Loneliness

ભ

I DARE SAY THAT AT THE ROOT of so many contemporary situations is a kind of impoverishment born of a widespread and radical sense of loneliness. Running after the latest fad, accumulating "friends" on one of the social networks, we get caught up in what contemporary society has to offer: loneliness—with fear of commitment—in a limitless effort to feel recognized.

~Address, Meeting with Bishops,
Philadelphia, September 27, 2015

Reflection: You can have many "friends" and still feel lonely because you may know that your friends like you in a very shallow way. Deep down, many people are very lonely and try to make up for that loneliness by attempting to feel loved or appreciated in superficial or silly ways.

True friendship takes time as we discover what we share with others—the same tastes, for example, or the same weird sense of humor. But being a true friend means that we spend time listening to them, being with them, maybe consoling them.

The beauty of friendship is that we can offer it first, and by offering it we may discover a cure for our own loneliness and someone else's.

August 2

Goodness Is Strength

ભ

GOODNESS IS NEVER WEAK but rather shows its strength by refusing to take revenge.

~Address, Meeting with Children at a
Charitable Center, Tirana, Albania, September 21, 2014

Reflection: Isaac Newton's third law of motion states, "For every action, there is an equal and opposite reaction."

In human relations, too, there is a natural tendency to react. Revenge is part of a reaction; it is hard to resist it, and it takes strength and courage to avoid revenge. Which is precisely why resistance is the greater and better course of action.

August 3

Promoting Dignity

CR

BEING A CHRISTIAN ENTAILS promoting the dignity of our brothers and sisters, fighting for it, living for it. That is why Christians are constantly called to set aside their own wishes and desires, their pursuit of power, before the concrete gaze of those who are most vulnerable.

~Homily, Havana, Cuba, September 20, 2015

Reflection: Lots of parents wake up in the middle of the night, worried about their children. They can't just relax and enjoy themselves if they know their children are in danger or suffering somewhere. They may be tired, but their concern is stronger than their fatigue.

Being a Christian means being given a new family; I cannot simply pursue my own wishes or importance when I know God's children—my brothers and sisters—are suffering. Lord, help me remember all of your family every day!

August 4

We Are Called to Serve First

CR

ALL OF US ARE ASKED, INDEED URGED, by Jesus to care for one another out of love. Without looking to one side or the other to see what our neighbor is doing or not doing. Jesus says, "Whoever would be first among you must be the last, and the servant of all." That person will be the first.

Jesus does not say, if your neighbor wants to be first, let him be the servant! We have to be careful to avoid judgmental looks and renew our belief in the transforming look to which Jesus invites us.

~Homily, Havana, Cuba,
September 20, 2015

Reflection: When I ask my children to do chores, often they will say, "But what about X [sibling]—what does he have to do?" We're always so worried about everyone else. But my kids don't usually ask me, "What about X?" when I give them something special (even if they decide to share it).

We think that serving is a burden, when it is actually a privilege. If we listen or read the words of people who have worked extensively with the poor and handicapped, such as Mother Teresa or Jean Vanier, we realize what a great opportunity it is. Let's not waste it!

August 5

The Family Is for All Ages

CR

STRESSING THE IMPORTANCE OF THE FAMILY not only helps to give direction and hope to new generations, but also to many of our elderly who are often forced to live alone and are effectively abandoned because there is no longer the warmth of a family hearth able to accompany and support them.

~Address to Members of the European Parliament, Strasbourg, France, November 25, 2014

Reflection: We know that children cannot live on their own; they are physically unable to care for themselves and they (like all of us) need companionship to thrive. So good parents look out for their children. Some older people aren't able to care for themselves, and we may care for those needs, too, when we become aware of them. But often, we don't take older people's need for companionship seriously; we don't recognize their desire to be part of a family for their entire lives.

So many older people—many of whom spent their lives caring for their own children and grandchildren, are deprived of family life when their kids grow up. It's as if the world moved on and left them behind. No one—child or adult—should be left behind. We are never too old to need company.

Can I give the gift of my presence to a lonely older person? How can I make someone who feels alone be part of my family?

August 6

Family Cross—and Resurrection

ભ

CERTAINLY, IN THE FAMILY THERE ARE DIFFICULTIES. In families we argue.... Families always, always, have crosses. Always....

But in families also, the cross is followed by resurrection, because there too the Son of God leads us. So the family is—if you excuse the word—a workshop of hope, of the hope of life and resurrection.

~Address, Prayer Vigil, Philadelphia,
September 26, 2015

Reflection: We live in a world of disposable objects: things we use and throw out. More and more, things are built for what is called "planned obsolescence," where the manufacturers expect you to get rid of the product and upgrade after a certain amount of time.

Many people treat their relationships the same way: you're friends because you're in the same class, at the same workplace, or have kids the same age. But then, when things change, you move on and leave those people behind. In a world like ours, especially, just holding on to things and to people is an amazing sign of hope to the world.

Many times, family life is difficult. We fight, we're unkind to one another, we bear the terrible burdens of sickness and sin. But the very fact that we stay, that we remain together, that we don't abandon one another, is a sign of something great—something that lasts, that endures in the world.

Whatever goes wrong, our faithfulness, our continuing to love and keep trying makes our homes workshops of hope.

August 7
Awake to Others' Needs

ℭℛ

LET US LEARN FROM MARY to keep our hearts awake and attentive to the needs of others. As the wedding feast of Cana teaches us, let us be concerned for the little details of life, and let us not tire of praying for one another, so that no one will lack the new wine of love, the joy which Jesus brings us.

~Angelus, September 20, 2015

Reflection: When we think of Jesus' miracles we usually think of his curing the sick, raising the dead, or driving out demons. But Jesus' first miracle was at a party—and it was his mother's suggestion. He didn't want the family's joy to be any less because they didn't provide enough wine; this apparently small detail was a big deal for him.

The first thing Jesus does is to bring unexpected joy and blessing—in both big things and small details.

August 8

Joy Springs from a Grateful Heart

CR

THE JOY OF MEN AND WOMEN who love God attracts others to him.... Joy springs from a grateful heart. Truly, we have received much, so many graces, so many blessings, and we rejoice in this.

~Homily, Vespers, New York City,
September 25, 2015

Reflection: "Rejoice in the Lord, always," St. Paul told the Philippians. But what does it mean to rejoice when things are going badly—either in the world, or for you personally?

St. Paul went to prison more than once, and he experienced his share of personal challenges before being beheaded. Joy isn't happiness: it's a gladness that comes from knowing that this world isn't all there is, and that the goodness of God has entered the world for good.

Life will have its ups and downs, but we can always, *always* rejoice in the Lord, for he is good, and his mercy endures forever.

August 9

Leaving Everything Behind

CR

THE SPIRIT OF POVERTY, the spirit of detachment, the spirit of leaving everything behind in order to follow Jesus: this leaving everything is not something I am inventing. It appears frequently in the Gospel. In the calling of the first ones who left their boat, their nets, and followed him. Those who left everything to follow Jesus.

~Address, Vespers, Havana, Cuba,
September 20, 2015

Reflection: Leaving everything to follow Jesus sounds crazy—and unnecessary. But whenever we love someone, there comes a time when we are forced to choose between that love and something (or someone) else. Jesus offers himself as the one thing we truly need, the one person who is essential to our happiness.

Sooner or later, we will be asked to make a choice between Christ and all the rest. The more we learn his value, the more we learn the spirit of poverty, which allows us entry to the greatest riches we can imagine.

August 10

He Helps Us Get Back on Track

ॐ

GOD, WHEN HE FORGIVES US, he accompanies us and helps us along the way. Always. Even in the small things. When we go to confession, the Lord tells us: "I forgive you. But now come with me." And he helps us to get back on the path.

He never condemns. He never simply forgives, but he forgives and accompanies. Then we are fragile, and we have to return to confession, everyone. But he never tires. He always takes us by the hand again. This is the love of God.

~Address to Prisoners and Staff, Penitentiary,
Castrovillari, Italy, June 21, 2014

Reflection: When you walk with a small child, you often get places very slowly—even if they like to run—because many children like to wander. That's one of the reasons we walk with them and often take their hands. We hold children's hands to keep them safe, and also to keep them on the right path.

In many ways, we are like children. We take a long time getting to God because we wander so easily. Christ came to guide us, to teach us, to die for us. But the first and greatest gift is his presence: Emmanuel means God with us. He is *with* us, not just pointing the way, but going with us.

And that makes all the difference.

August 11

Little Things Mean a Lot

℘

"MAY I?", "THANK YOU," AND "PARDON ME" ... these expressions open up the way to living well in your family, to living in peace. They are simple expressions, but not so simple to put into practice! They hold much power: the power to keep home life intact even when tested with a thousand problems.

But if they are absent, little holes can start to crack open and the whole thing may even collapse.

~General Audience, May 13, 2015

Reflection: Many parents are very insistent when they teach their children manners. Sometimes, if children don't say please, a parent will remind them, "What's the magic word?" It's easy to feel taken for granted in family life; it's easy to feel like people don't care what you think or do, or even feel sorry when they do mistreat you.

When people get stuck feeling that way, it becomes difficult for them to treat others well ... and a cycle develops that can be hard to get out of. Sometimes, we don't know where to begin, but we can begin with these small acts of courtesy, expressed sincerely. They really are magic words—if we use them intentionally.

August 12

Prayer Unites Us

☙

PRAYER UNITES US; IT MAKES US BROTHERS AND SISTERS. It opens our hearts and reminds us of a beautiful truth which we sometimes forget. In prayer, we all learn to say, "Father," "Dad." And when we say, "Father," "Dad," we learn to see one another as brothers and sisters.

In prayer, there are no rich or poor, there are sons and daughters, sisters and brothers. In prayer, there is no first- or second-class, there is brotherhood.

~Address, Charitable Center, St. Patrick Parish,
Washington, D.C., September 24, 2015

Reflection: If we take a good look at the world, God seems pretty extravagant. It seems like he wanted so many different kinds of things—so many varieties of plants and animals, so many different geological formations, so many different kinds of people. This is an amazing thing—but also difficult, because it sometimes overwhelms and confuses us.

This is true in our families as well: We probably would not have chosen some of the people who have been given to us to be put in our lives. Our families are a great place for seeing that very different—even difficult!—people have been given to us to know and love.

And, in prayer, we begin to understand that all the people of the world are God's children, also given to us to know and love.

August 13

Offering Everyone the Life of Jesus

CR

LET US GO OUT, LET US GO FORTH to offer everyone the life of Jesus Christ (cf. *Evangelii Gaudium*, 49). The People of God can embrace everyone because we are the disciples of the One who knelt before his own to wash their feet.

~Homily, Canonization Mass of Junípero Serra,
Washington, D.C., September 23, 2015

Reflection: If you've ever lived in a busy, dusty city in the summertime and worn sandals or flip-flops a lot, you know just how dirty your feet can get. Given the condition of Jerusalem in Jesus' day, we can imagine there was probably more than just dust caked on his disciples' feet.

The washing of the feet is one of the only times Jesus specifically tells his disciples they should imitate him: there is nobody or nothing too gross for him. And there shouldn't be for us either, if we're looking to imitate him.

Lord, help us love as you do!

August 14

The Eye of Glass

☙

A LATIN AMERICAN WRITER ONCE SAID that we all have two eyes: one of flesh and another of glass. With the eye of flesh, we see what is in front of us. With the eye of glass, we see what we dream of. Beautiful, isn't it?

In the daily reality of life, there has to be room for dreaming. A young person incapable of dreaming is cut off, self-enclosed. Everyone sometimes dreams of things which are never going to happen. But dream them anyway, desire them, seek new horizons, be open to great things.

~Address to Students, Havana, Cuba,
September 20, 2015

Reflection: In the Old Testament, dreams often came as a gift from God and showed the dreamer something he did not fully understand. Nowadays, when we talk about dreams, usually we are thinking of daydreams, of our hopes and desires.

We can learn a lot from these dreams, too, because they can show us the deepest desire of our heart. We may think we know what we want, but if we pay attention, we often find that our greatest longings aren't quite what we planned or expected.

August 15

Tender Mercies

Ↄ

HAPPY ARE THE MERCIFUL. Happy are those who know how to put themselves in someone else's shoes, those who are able to embrace, to forgive.

We have all experienced this at one time or another. And how beautiful it is! It is like getting our lives back, getting a new chance. Nothing is more beautiful than to have a new chance. It is as if life can start all over again.

~Address, Meeting with Young People,
Asunción, Paraguay, July 12, 2015

Reflection: Once, I cracked my phone screen very badly in a weird accident. My phone was completely out of warranty and I had no hope it could be repaired. I knew I had no claim for a replacement phone: the accident had been my own fault, and I had no service plan or insurance to cover a replacement. But when I went to the service center, they surprised me by giving me a new phone. I felt such a rush of gratitude: a second chance!

We give people a new chance when we forgive them—even though they "don't deserve it"—we don't, either! In forgiving people and giving them space to start over, we start over again, which is a gift to others and to ourselves.

August 16

New Homes and New Friends

❧

I KNOW THAT IT IS NOT EASY to have to move and find a new home, to meet new neighbors and new friends. It is not easy, but you have to start. At the beginning it can be pretty hard....

The good thing is that we also make new friends. This is very important, the new friends we make. We meet people who open doors for us, who are kind to us. They offer us friendship and understanding, and they try to help us not to feel like strangers.

~Address, Meeting with Immigrant Families,
Harlem, New York, September 25, 2015

Reflection: Being a stranger is never fun. Even if we've lived in the same place for a while, we know what it feels like: being at a party where you don't know anyone else, starting a new job or at a new school.

But when we go to new places, we also meet new people. And those new people remind us that we're not really alone, and we often discover great new friendships; our circles—and our hearts—expand.

August 17

The Common Good

ભ

IN BUENOS AIRES, IN A NEW PARISH in an extremely poor area, a group of university students were building some rooms for the parish. So the parish priest said to me, "Why don't you come one Saturday and I'll introduce them to you." They were building on Saturdays and Sundays. They were young men and women from the university.

So I arrived, I saw them, and they were introduced to me: "This is the architect. He's Jewish. This one is Communist. This one is a practicing Catholic." They were all different, yet they were all working for the common good.

This is called social friendship, where everyone works for the common good.

~Address to Students, Havana, Cuba,
September 20, 2015

Reflection: "Necessity is the mother of invention," the saying goes. Necessity can also be the mother of unity. When people see others in need, and move forward to address those needs, they discover bonds with people who seemed very different—even hostile—to them.

In building what is good, I discover people who are surprisingly good as well.

August 18

Rebuilding Families

℅

WE ALL KNOW FAMILIES that have divided siblings, who have quarreled. Let us ask the Lord—perhaps in our family there are a few cases—to help these families to reunite their siblings, to rebuild the family.

~General Audience, February 18, 2015

Reflection: I know people who only discovered that they had an aunt—or an uncle—when a grandparent died and someone they didn't know showed up at the funeral! In some families, the conflicts go so deep that someone's very existence was never acknowledged.

Even if we haven't taken things to that extreme, sometimes our hurts and resentments divide us and create even more damage. Whatever terrible things someone has done, God does not want this. We need an experience of his mercy so that we can start to let go of the resentments that harden and close our hearts.

August 19

Beautiful World; Beautiful God

CR

GOD IS CERTAINLY TRUTH, God is certainly good, God certainly knows how to make things, he created the world. But above all, God is beautiful! The beauty of God. So often we forget about beauty! Mankind thinks, feels, makes, but is in such need today of beauty.

~General Audience, January 7, 2015

Reflection: One of the great things about beauty is that we can't fully understand it—which is why it's such a great sign of God! When something or someone is beautiful, it can be hard to explain why, but we just want to share that experience of beauty with others, by showing them the sunset, or introducing them to someone, or playing them a song. That beauty helps draw me to the One who made such a beautiful world.

Lord, help me to see and share your beauty; let me see you more clearly in all that is beautiful.

August 20

A Better Future for the Whole World

☙

YOUNG PEOPLE DEMAND CHANGE. They wonder how anyone can claim to be building a better future without thinking of the environmental crisis and the sufferings of the excluded [the poor].

~Laudato Si', 13

Reflection: Everyone gets used to seeing the same problems, and so we all learn to tune things out. One of the gifts of young eyes is that they notice things we older people have stopped paying attention to. We can't try to build a better world without addressing the biggest problems: the earth itself and its poorest inhabitants.

Can I look at the biggest problems in life with eyes full of hope—and compassion?

August 21
Side by Side

CB

LET US GO SIDE BY SIDE WITH ONE ANOTHER, as one. Encountering one another, even though we may think differently, even though we may feel differently.

~Address to Students, Havana, Cuba,
September 20, 2015

Reflection: Traveling with someone new is always a risk—and an adventure. Part of the adventure is the new place, and part of it is the new person. We recognize that traveling means seeing new and beautiful places—but also dealing with some inevitable hassles.

Can we see that new people, whatever their limitations or aggravating qualities, bring us something beautiful and new as well—that they, too, offer us new and dazzling landscapes?

August 22

Follow in Mary's Footsteps

ℭ

WHEN THE CHURCH LOOKS FOR JESUS, she always knocks at his mother's door and asks, "Show us Jesus." It is from Mary that the Church learns true discipleship. That is why the Church always goes out on mission in the footsteps of Mary.

~Homily, Shrine of Our Lady of Aparecida,
Brazil, July 24, 2013

Reflection: Jesus was human and divine: both God and Man. Mary was without sin, but she was only human. This is one of the great reasons that she is such a help to us in going to her Son.

Her body was the place where the human and divine came together—she knows the joy of that, just like any mother knows the joy of her child kicking in her womb. Mary is always looking for ways to bring the human and divine together in all our lives. We can always be sure of our path when we walk in her footsteps.

Mary, help us walk in your ways of humility and peace.

August 23

Understanding the Signs of the Times

ભ

FOR UNDERSTANDING THE SIGNS OF THE TIMES ... silence is necessary: to be quiet, to watch and observe. And afterwards to think within ourselves. For example: Why are there so many wars now? Why did this thing happen? And to pray. [Therefore] silence, reflection and prayer. Only then can we understand the signs of the times and what Jesus wants to tell us.

~Homily, *Domus Sanctae Marthae*,
October 23, 2015

Reflection: It can be difficult to keep quiet—especially for some of us. But when we are curious, when we are excited, when it's important, we know how to stay silent—like when we're watching a great movie or trying to sneak past a sleeping child or parent.

Paying attention takes time; we have to be patient. But if we give silence some space in our lives, we will be amazed at everything we start to notice, how much more we understand and appreciate the world around us.

August 24

The Family Lives on a Promise

ভ

ONE COULD SAY THAT THE FAMILY lives on the promise of love and fidelity that a man and a woman make to one another. This includes the commitment to welcome and raise their children; but it is also carried out in caring for elderly parents, in protecting and tending to the weakest members of the family, in helping each other develop their own qualities and accept their own limitations.

~General Audience, October 28, 2015

Reflection: American children often hear the story of Johnny Appleseed, who went around the country sowing apple seeds, changing the American landscape forever. Seeds seem so small, so insignificant, but they leave a long legacy.

It's true in marriage, as well: many married couples struggle; they fight; they make many mistakes. And yet, over time, their faithfulness allows so much to take root: it nurtures a commitment to caring for young and old alike, in bringing out the greatness in people, despite—and even through—their limitations.

Do I see the fruit of faithfulness in my life and that of others? Can I cultivate more patience to let it take root in my life?

August 25

Jesus Wanted Kids Around

૭

DEAR CHILDREN, I WANT TO ASK YOU A QUESTION; maybe you can help me. They tell me that you are all very intelligent, and so I want to ask you: Did Jesus ever get annoyed?... Do you remember when?

If this seems like a difficult question, let me help you. It was when they wouldn't let the children come to him. That is the only time in the entire Gospel of Mark when we hear that he was "annoyed" (cf. Mk 10:13-15). We would say that he was really "ticked off."

Do you get annoyed every now and then? Jesus felt that way when they wouldn't let the children come to him. He was really mad. He loved children. Not that he didn't like adults, but he was really happy to be with children. He enjoyed their company; he enjoyed being friends with them.

But not only. He didn't just want to have them around, he wanted something else: he wanted them to be an example. He told his disciples that "unless you become like children, you will never enter the kingdom of heaven" (Mt 18:3).

~Address to Sick Children, Asunción,
Paraguay, July 11, 2015

Reflection: What does it mean to be an example? It means other people can learn from you. So why does Jesus want us to follow children—usually children follow older people.

One reason Jesus wants us to imitate children is because they aren't afraid to admit they need help, or love, or company, or someone to follow. They aren't worried about living up to expectations.

We can learn to be simple and also learn to be honest about what we truly need. But letting go of our image of ourselves is hard sometimes. Let's have the courage to let ourselves be small again.

August 26

He Believes in You

℘

IF GOD HIMSELF ENTERED OUR HISTORY and became flesh in Jesus, if he shouldered our weakness and sin, then you need not be afraid of hope, or of the future, because God is on your side. He believes in you, and he hopes in you.

~Address to Students, Havana, Cuba,
September 20, 2015

Reflection: If God is with us, who can be against us? The Good Thief asked Jesus to remember him as they were both dying on their crosses, and Jesus promised him that he would be with him in paradise. Jesus had never met him before, but believed his sincerity and recognized his desire.

He believes in us just as much!

August 27

Like a Sibling, Ready to Serve

ભ

LET US ASK THE LORD TO MAKE US more brotherly and sisterly among ourselves, and more ready to serve our needier brothers and sisters.
~General Audience, October 28, 2015

Reflection: The anthropologist Margaret Mead noted the importance of older siblings in many cultures and how important older children were in so many places through the world; an importance that is often lost in contemporary society.

Older siblings help out, they care for their younger brothers and sisters, they do some of the work that would otherwise fall heavily on the parents, especially in larger families.

But younger siblings are also crucial: their sweetness softens the hearts of their older siblings as well as their parents, they make people feel appreciated and loved for who they are. Lord, let us see the needy among us as true brothers and sisters in you!

August 28

American Dreams

CR

AMERICA CONTINUES TO BE, FOR MANY, a land of "dreams." Dreams which lead to action, to participation, to commitment. Dreams which awaken what is deepest and truest in the life of a people.

~Address, Joint Session of U.S. Congress,
September 24, 2015

Reflection: When Americans think of their country, they often think of a "land of opportunity," of a place that inspired members of their family to leave their native land in search of a better life.

Whether those dreams became reality or not, they inspired concrete action, and it is that spirit—of desiring something greater, and taking the necessary risks to make it happen—that reveals the greatness of a people.

August 29

Jesus Precedes Us

CR

JESUS GOES BEFORE US, he precedes us; he opens the way and invites us to follow him. He invites us slowly to overcome ... our reluctance to think that others, much less ourselves, can change.

~Homily, Mass, Holguín, Cuba,
September 21, 2015

Reflection: "You first" we often say to people when we've agreed to do something but we're not sure we want to. It gives us courage and confidence when someone else takes the initiative.

Jesus has gone first. He's been through all the hardest moments already. He is ready to change our hearts and gives us hope even in our darkest hour.

August 30

He's Asking You to Knock on Doors, Too

ભ

TODAY CHRIST IS KNOCKING AT THE DOOR OF YOUR HEART, of my heart. He calls you and me to rise, to be wide-awake and alert, and to see the things in life that really matter.

What is more, he is asking you and me to go out on the highways and byways of this world, knocking on the doors of other people's hearts, inviting them to welcome him into their lives.

~Address, Meeting with Asian Youth,
Dangjin, South Korea, August 15, 2014

Reflection: When we hear a knock on the door, we usually feel moved to get up and answer it—that is, unless we think we know who it is and don't want to see them. Is that how we see Jesus? Or have we realized that Christ is the answer to what we desire most in life—he is the one we've been waiting for our whole lives.

He will keep knocking until we answer. Once we do—once we realize all that he truly is—*we* will start knocking on doors, because why would we keep such an amazing discovery to ourselves?

August 31

Letting Ourselves Love and Be Loved

☙

CHILDREN HAVE THE CAPACITY TO SMILE AND TO CRY. Some, when I pick them up to embrace them, smile; others see me dressed in white and think I am a doctor and that I am going to vaccinate them, and they cry ... spontaneously! Children are like this: they smile and cry, two things which are often "stifled" in grown-ups....

So often our smile becomes a cardboard smile, fixed, a smile that is not natural, even an artificial smile, like a clown. Children smile spontaneously and cry spontaneously. It always depends on the heart, and often our heart is blocked and loses this capacity to smile, to cry. So children can teach us how to smile and cry again.

~General Audience, March 18, 2015

Reflection: Have you ever had the experience of seeing someone smile in your direction—and you smile back, thinking the smile is for you until you realize the person is smiling at someone else? It can be embarrassing. Somehow, we feel like smiling is a risk. And crying is just totally embarrassing!

But so what if we smile at people and cry sometimes? When we smile, we are showing people we are open to loving them. When we cry, we show that we also need to be loved by them. Those are good things, even if they feel embarrassing sometimes. Lord, don't let me be too embarrassed to love and be loved.

September 1

Praying to a Friend

ᴄᴙ

Aʀᴇ ʏᴏᴜ ᴘʀᴀʏɪɴɢ? Do you know that you can speak with Jesus, with the Father, with the Holy Spirit, as you speak to a friend? And not just any friend, but the greatest and most trusted of your friends!
~Message for the Thirtieth World Youth Day, 2015

Reflection: Prayer is our first and greatest gift from God, because he's always there, listening, even when it doesn't seem like it. We don't need to find special words—we just need to tell him what's on our mind and in our heart, even though he already knows.

He is constantly ready and waiting to give us the gift of himself—but we have to ask.

September 2

A Tender Revolution

CR

DAY AFTER DAY, we are asked to renew our faith. We are asked to live the revolution of tenderness as Mary, our Mother of Charity, did. We are invited ... to open our eyes and hearts to others.

Our revolution comes about through tenderness, through the joy which always becomes closeness and compassion—which is not pity, but "suffering with" ... and leads us to get involved in, and to serve, the life of others.

~Homily, Mass, Santiago, Cuba,
September 22, 2015

Reflection: Revolution is a strong word. It brings up images of battle and bloodshed. But the word was first used to refer to celestial bodies (planets and so forth) and how they moved around the sun.

What do we move around—what makes us move and live? Can we learn, like Mary, to live our lives moving in relation to Jesus? There we will find a tenderness that changes us more than battle and bloodshed ever could, a tenderness that unites us to others in their suffering—and their joy.

September 3

Faithful to Our Word

ℭ

FAITHFULNESS TO PROMISES is a true masterpiece of humanity!…
Honoring the word given, fidelity to the promise, cannot be bought and sold. They cannot be compelled by force or shielded without sacrifice.

~General Audience, October 21, 2015

Reflection: In many societies it was said that "a man's word was his honor": keeping promises was one of the most important values on both an individual and social level. Jesus, too, exhorts us to "say yes when we mean yes and no when we mean no." This is harder than it sounds!

Being true to my word forces me to think carefully about what I commit to; it saves me from saying yes when I don't mean it. And it also compels me to make sacrifices when changing my mind would be easier than following through. Faithfulness to our promises is no small thing: it is a great one.

Lord, help me to be true to my small promises so that I may learn faithfulness in greater ones as well.

September 4

You Won't Be Disappointed

CR

WHERE JESUS IS THERE IS HOPE; where Jesus is there is love for brothers and sisters, there is the commitment to safeguarding their life and their health, and to respecting the environment and nature.

This is the hope that never disappoints, the hope which Jesus gives!

~Homily, Mass, Caserta, Italy, July 26, 2014

Reflection: If someone lends us something, we often treat it better than if it were our own. Somehow, we may realize its value better when it belongs to someone else. Jesus knows that things are his own, but they are also his Father's. Do we realize that the people we meet and the world we live in belong to him? Do we treat them that way?

September 5

The Power of Christ in Our Hearts

CR

THERE IS NO FORCE MORE POWERFUL than the one released from the hearts of young people when they have been conquered by the experience of friendship with [Jesus]. Christ has confidence in young people and entrusts them with the very future of his mission: "Go and make disciples." Go beyond the confines of what is humanly possible and create a world of brothers and sisters!

~Address, Welcome Ceremony, World Youth Day,
Rio de Janeiro, Brazil, July 22, 2013

Reflection: Some people dream of having superpowers: being invisible, having X-ray vision. St. Peter was a young man when Jesus met him, and when he trusted in Christ he was able to walk on water. It was only when he started to think about himself that he sank.

It's the same for us, especially if we're young and have natural enthusiasm and energy to add to Christ's grace! Just like Peter, Christ calls us all to be "fishers of men," to bring him to all people, enabled by the force of our own hearts, strengthened in his love.

September 6

Jesus Isn't Picky

◌঩

IT IS INTERESTING TO SEE HOW JESUS ... shows up at meals, at dinners. Eating with different people, visiting different homes was a special way for him to make known God's plan. He goes to the home of his friends, Martha and Mary, but he is not choosy; it makes no difference to him whether publicans or sinners are there.

~Address, Meeting with Families,
Santiago, Cuba, September 22, 2015

Reflection: When we sit down and eat we get a real chance to encounter people—we get to know them, we find out their likes and dislikes, we even try new food. Mealtimes are a great moment for us to remember that we need companionship as well as food in order to live. In our lives, are we scrounging around for something to eat, or are we ready to sit down for a meal?

September 7

He Seeks Us Out

ॐ

JESUS IS AMONG US; he is here today. He said, "When you are gathered in my name, I am among you." The Lord is here, he is with us, he is in our midst! It is he who seeks us; it is he who lets himself be found even by those who do not seek him.

At times he allows himself to be found in unusual places and at unexpected times.

~Homily, Mass, Caserta, Italy, July 26, 2014

Reflection: There is a famous story of a boy who plays hide and seek, but no one comes to find him. The storyteller suggests that this is how God feels—no one looks for him. And yet, Christ upsets that dynamic, because he comes to get us; Jesus is always with us. Even when we aren't looking for him, he's looking for us.

When we truly believe he is with us, we start finding him in some of the most surprising moments and places. Will we look for him? And will we allow him to find us?

September 8

A Mother for All Seasons

ଔ

MARY IS MOTHER, SHE ALWAYS ASSISTS US: when we are working and when we are looking for work, when we have clear ideas and when we are confused, when prayer flows spontaneously and when the heart is desolate. She is always there to help us.

~Address, Meeting with Young People,
Castelpetroso, Italy, July 5, 2014

Reflection: Being a mother never ends; any mother who has lost a child knows this painful truth. A mother's love isn't conditional: a mother loves her child in all circumstances, joyful and painful.

Mary is a perfect mother and therefore is always available to us, even when our own natural mothers are far away or unable to be with us. She is also there to encourage and sustain us when we feel weary in our ability to love: all we need to do is ask.

Will you call upon your mother?

September 9

Families Sustain Us in Adversity

❧

WITHOUT FAMILY, WITHOUT THE WARMTH OF HOME, life grows empty, there is a weakening of the networks which sustain us in adversity, the networks which nurture us in daily living and motivate us to build a better future.

~Address, Meeting with Families,
Santiago, Cuba, September 22, 2015

Reflection: Building family life takes work. It helps to remember that the relationships that we build with our family members will nurture us all every day, even when we leave the home. The habits we learn in our family sustain us when life challenges us, both now and later.

September 10

Love Is Something to Live and Learn

CR

PERFECT FAMILIES DO NOT EXIST. This must not discourage us, quite the opposite. Love is something we learn; love is something we live; love grows as it is "forged" by the concrete situations which each particular family experiences.

Love is born and constantly develops amid lights and shadows.

~Address, Prayer Vigil,
Philadelphia, September 26, 2015

Reflection: We may feel bad, sometimes, that our families aren't perfect—or that they aren't a whole lot better: kinder, more obedient, more capable, you name it.

But love is our mission—it's a big deal! Do we really think we're going to spend our whole lives on something we can master so easily? Would you want to spend your whole life doing something that didn't get more interesting—and more challenging?

Lord, help us not to feel overwhelmed by the difficulties we experience in our families. Let us recognize our challenges as ways in which you are forging new and better hearts within us.

September 11

Greater Love

CR

HERE [AT THE GROUND ZERO MEMORIAL IN NEW YORK CITY] ... we have a palpable sense of the heroic goodness which people are capable of, those hidden reserves of strength from which we can draw. In the depths of pain and suffering ... hands reached out, lives were given....

No one thought about race, nationality, neighborhoods, religion, or politics. It was all about solidarity, meeting immediate needs, brotherhood. It was about being brothers and sisters. New York City firemen walked into the crumbling towers, with no concern for their own well-being. Many succumbed; their sacrifice enabled great numbers to be saved.

This place of death became a place of life, too, a place of saved lives, a hymn to the triumph of life over the prophets of destruction and death, to goodness over evil, to reconciliation and unity over hatred and division.

~Address, Ground Zero Memorial,
New York City, September 25, 2015

Reflection: A priest I know heard the confessions of many firemen before they entered the Twin Towers on 9/11. These men knew what was at stake, and they went anyway: ready to risk everything, to give everything, for love. Their sacrifice grieves us, but it also makes us glad, because they are a testament to the love that makes life worth living: a love infinitely greater than death.

September 12

Learning God's Language

ભ

KINDNESS AND THE ABILITY TO SAY "THANK YOU" are often considered a sign of weakness and raise the suspicion of others. This tendency is encountered even within the … family.…

A Christian who does not know how to thank has lost the very "language" of God. This is terrible! Let's not forget Jesus' question after he heals the ten lepers and only one of them returns to thank him (cf. Lk 17:18).

~General Audience, May 13, 2015

Reflection: We think of saying thank you as good manners—and it is. But it's not just good for the people being thanked; it's good for the people who say thank you as well, because they recognize what they've been given.

Jesus didn't care about manners for manners' sake. But when only one leper came back to thank him, he realized that the others didn't realize the true greatness of what happened to them. He was sorry for them, and we should be sorry for ourselves when we don't give thanks.

September 13

He Remembers

CB

GOD HAS A MEMORY; HE IS NOT FORGETFUL. God does not forget us; he always remembers. There is a passage in the Bible, from the prophet Isaiah, which says: Even should a mother forget her child—which is impossible—I will never forget you (cf. Is 49:15).

And this is true: God thinks about me. God remembers me. I am in God's memory.

~Address, Penitentiary, Isernia, Italy,
July 5, 2014

Reflection: Isaiah says that God won't forget us, "even should a mother forget her nursing child." When a mother breast-feeds a baby, her own body reminds her of her child's existence; she often realizes on her own that it's time to feed her infant, even if the baby doesn't cry (but especially if the baby does!).

It would seem impossible for a nursing mother to forget her child—and this same intensity characterizes the way God remembers us. He doesn't remember us because we are on his to-do list or because he writes notes to himself. He remembers because he chose to unite himself to us in his very existence.

And we think he could forget? We may not understand how he operates—but he never forgets.

September 14

Mercy for Those Suffering Invisible Death Penalties

CR

LIFE IMPRISONMENT IS A KIND OF CONCEALED DEATH PENALTY.... You are there, dying daily without the hope of ever being freed.

~In-flight Press Conference from
Cuba to the United States, September 22, 2015

Reflection: Visiting prisoners is a corporal work of mercy—even so, how many of us have done this in our lifetimes, let alone regularly? Being in jail for a long period of time can be a daily death. It is worth realizing that, in addition to prisoners themselves, there are many people in the world who feel imprisoned by psychological illnesses or other diseases.

Comforting the sick is also a work of mercy: let us seek out people we know who are trapped by jail, illness, or sin and bring them what companionship and comfort we can.

September 15

Grateful for Life and Parents

␣

LET US ALL THINK ABOUT OUR PARENTS and thank God for the gift of life. In silence, those who have children think of them, and everyone think of our parents. May the Lord bless our parents and … children.

~General Audience, February 11, 2015

Reflection: I only exist because someone else (my mother) let me live inside her. Someone else shielded me from danger and damage, fed me from her own body before I was born. The very fact that we are alive is a reason to be grateful, not just for life, but for the life that someone else made possible.

Lord, help me to be grateful to you, and grateful also for my parents.

September 16

The Courage to Say I'm Sorry

CR

A HOUSE IN WHICH THE WORDS "I'M SORRY" are never uttered begins to lack air, and the floodwaters begin to choke those who live inside. So many wounds, so many scrapes and bruises are the result of a lack of these precious words: "I am sorry."

~General Audience, May 13, 2015

Reflection: Why is it so hard to say sorry? Sometimes we think of apologizing as a weakness: the person of *lower* rank has to say sorry.

That may be true about saying sorry socially. But a true apology is an act of love, and in just the same way that it takes courage to express love to someone who may not love us back, it takes courage to say "I'm sorry" when we don't know if we'll be forgiven.

It takes strength to apologize. Let's not back down from the challenge.

September 17
Children Are a Good Sign

CR

CHILDREN ARE A SIGN. They are a sign of hope, a sign of life, but also a "diagnostic" sign, a marker indicating the health of families, society, and the entire world.

Wherever children are accepted, loved, cared for, and protected, the family is healthy ... and the world is more human.

~Homily, Mass, Bethlehem, Pilgrimage
to the Holy Land, May 25, 2014

Reflection: Staying healthy seems like a simple thing, but it takes work even for "healthy" people! We need to eat right, exercise, get outside. Sometimes, we work so hard to get healthier that we don't notice how healthy we are, and how good that is. Some of the signs of health are quiet: you don't hear people's breathing (because it's not heavy!), you don't hear them coughing (because they don't have a cough).

It's the same with our spiritual health. We may be busy getting our families and ourselves healthier, but let's stop to recognize the great blessing of our spiritual health. The very fact of having children, of loving them, of protecting them, of caring for them in our lives is a great sign of health.

Whatever our limitations, our families are a great sign to the world of something greater.

September 18

Words That Hurt

CR

HOW MUCH HARM WORDS DO when they are motivated by feelings of jealousy and envy! To speak ill of others puts them in a bad light, undermines their reputation, and leaves them prey to the whims of gossip.

~*Misericordiae Vultus*, Bull of Indiction
for the Year of Mercy, 14

Reflection: Everyone wonders—and most people worry—about what others think of them. Talking badly of other people often helps us feel better about ourselves, it distracts us from our own fears. But it also makes the world an uglier place and hurts everyone.

Can we learn to be honest about our own motivation when we bad-mouth people? Lord, help me to see the truth in others—and in myself.

September 19

No Need to Settle

ભ

THE SPIRIT OF THE WORLD tells us to be like everyone else, to settle for what comes easy. Faced with this human way of thinking, "we must regain the conviction that we need one another, that we have a shared responsibility for others and for the world" (cf. *Laudato Si'*, 229).

It is the responsibility to proclaim the message of Jesus.

~Homily, Canonization Mass of Junípero Serra,
Washington, D.C., September 23, 2015

Reflection: There are some people whose lives are busy, and who say that they don't have enough time for friendship. The spirit of the world can affect us in many ways. We may have many important things to do, but the people in the world are no less worthy of our attention.

Christ laid down his life for his friends, and he invites us to do the same for ours.

September 20

Courage to Face Problems

 CR

YOUNG PEOPLE ARE COURAGEOUS, I have said this, the young have hope and … the capacity for solidarity.…

Go forward with your brother and sister to help them overcome problems.

~Address, Meeting with Young People,
Castelpetroso, Italy, July 5, 2014

Reflection: Most people don't go looking for friends in order to find more problems—but in a way, that's what happens. More friends mean more problems, but it also means more fun, so we don't mind too much. The beauty of solidarity, of true friendship, is that we find the solutions as we find the problems, and so we don't feel the burden of our troubles the same way.

September 21

Proclaiming the Merciful Embrace of the Father

 obr

JESUS SAID: GO OUT AND TELL THE GOOD NEWS to everyone. Go out and in my name embrace life as it is, and not as you think it should be.

Go out to the highways and byways, go out to tell the good news fearlessly, without prejudice, without superiority, without condescension, to all those who have lost the joy of living.

Go out to proclaim the merciful embrace of the Father.

~Homily, Canonization Mass of Junípero Serra,
Washington, D.C., September 23, 2015

Reflection: Go out! Jesus tells us. Not tomorrow, not when we've figured things out, not when we're ready, not when we find people we think will listen to us, but *right now.*

We are being asked to bring the Good News to everyone we meet. They are free to accept or reject it, and we don't need to be afraid of that. But there is no time *but* the present, and he is already with us to help us.

September 22

May God Make Us Close to One Another

CR

LET US ASK GOD TO INCREASE OUR DESIRE to be close to one another. To be neighbors, always there for one another, with all our many differences, interests, and ways of seeing things.

To speak straightforwardly, despite our disagreements and disputes, and not behind each other's backs.

~Address, Vespers, Havana, Cuba,
September 20, 2015

Reflection: Most people fight more with their siblings than with their roommates or friends. Usually, it's because they know that their siblings are stuck with them, and so they are more honest, even when they disagree.

But the funny thing is, the relationship is usually stronger when we tell people what bothers us, when we try to work it out, despite the challenges.

Lord, increase our desire to be close to each other, and increase our trust that all things can be worked out.

September 23
¡Siempre Adelante!

ભ

JUNÍPERO SERRA LEFT HIS NATIVE LAND and its way of life. He was excited about blazing trails, going forth to meet many people, learning and valuing their particular customs and ways of life. He learned how to bring to birth and nurture God's life in the faces of everyone he met; he made them his brothers and sisters....

Father Serra had a motto which inspired his life and work.... *¡Siempre adelante!* Keep moving forward! For him, this was the way to continue experiencing the joy of the Gospel, to keep his heart from growing numb.

~Homily, Canonization Mass of Junípero Serra,
Washington, D.C., September 23, 2015

Reflection: People who move to a foreign country may feel very strange in their new home. Different culture, different habits, different language; there may by many things that feel strange. But if they come back home, they may suddenly feel out of place as well; they've been changed by the experience of living abroad.

The truth is that being Christian calls us to a bigger, grander idea of what it means to be home. We still love our own hometown and native people, but we know that home isn't just where we are from, but what we are moving toward.

Junípero Serra knew this, and it inspired a greatness of spirit that moved many to conversion. May we know this same greatness of spirit!

September 24

Sincerity and Truth

CHILDREN ARE NOT DIPLOMATS: they say what they feel, say what they see, directly. And so often they put their parents in difficulty, saying in front of other people, "I don't like this because it is ugly."

But children say what they see, they are not two-faced, they have not yet learned that science of duplicity that we adults have unfortunately learned.

~General Audience, March 18, 2015

Reflection: Children are famous for saying awkward truths, like in the story "The Emperor's New Clothes": a child blurts out the truth that the adults won't say because they are afraid of looking stupid. Grown-ups (as in the story) often tell lies because they are concerned with what other people will think of them if they tell the truth.

We can learn from children that being truthful and sincere is more important than presenting a particular image to the world—that image is an illusion. At the same time, we can teach children how to be gentle with the things they say, and how to love other people better in kindness, sincerity, *and* truth.

September 25
People, Not Numbers

☙

OUR WORLD IS FACING A REFUGEE CRISIS of a magnitude not seen since the Second World War. This presents us with great challenges and many hard decisions....

We must not be taken aback by their numbers, but rather view them as persons, seeing their faces and listening to their stories, trying to respond as best we can to their situation.... Let us remember the Golden Rule: "Do unto others as you would have them do unto you" (Mt 7:12).

~Address, Joint Session of U.S. Congress,
September 24, 2015

Reflection: Sometimes, if we're waiting for someone at a crowded public place such as a train station or an airport, we can feel overwhelmed by the mass of people. But when we see the face of the person we're looking for, all of a sudden the "crowd" subsides: we see a *person* instead of just a crowd.

This is the big challenge in the face of refugee crises as well: seeing the person and remembering that behind the "faceless" masses of people there are individuals who Christ has asked us to treat with love and dignity. This doesn't solve questions of public policy, but it orients our hearts and minds as we seek solutions that respect the vulnerable and suffering in their full personhood.

September 26

Money Isn't Happiness

CR

DO NOT FALL INTO THE TERRIBLE TRAP of thinking that life depends on money.... We cannot take money with us into the life beyond. Money does not bring us happiness.

~*Misericordiae Vultus*, Bull of Indiction
for the Year of Mercy, 19

Reflection: According to an old joke, a robber stopped a man at gunpoint and said, "Your money or your life." The victim replied, "My life; I'm saving my money for my old age."

We know we can't bring our money with us when we die, and we realize it doesn't bring us happiness ... and yet we often live as if we've forgotten those truths.

Because money can make life easier, more stable, buy us more of the things we like, and make other people respect us more, we figure it's still a pretty safe bet. But it's not a safe bet, and it's one of the ways the devil can seduce us into following him instead of following God.

Can I live in faith, confident that my happiness doesn't—or will not—come from money, but from God?

September 27

Family: Holiness in the Ordinary

അ

THE FAMILY IS A PLACE where evangelical holiness is lived out in the most ordinary conditions. There we are formed by the memory of past generations and we put down roots which enable us to go far.

The family is a place of discernment, where we learn to recognize God's plan for our lives and to embrace it with trust. It is a place of gratuitousness, of discreet fraternal presence and solidarity, a place where we learn to step out of ourselves and accept others, to forgive and to feel forgiven.

~Address, Prayer Vigil in Preparation
for the Synod of Bishops, October 3, 2015

Reflection: God loved us first, the pope often reminds us, and the family is a great reminder of this in the flesh: We were loved before we were even born. Then, in family life, we get to work out the details of what this means in practice: this can take a lot of work and a lot of time!

But having a place where this truth is truly made flesh is a great gift. It is a sign of God's boundless affection.

September 28

Childlike Simplicity and Purity

CR

[CHILDREN] BRING THEIR WAY OF SEEING REALITY, with a trusting and pure gaze. A child has spontaneous trust in his father and mother; he has spontaneous trust in God, in Jesus, in Our Lady.... We know that children are also marked by original sin, that they are selfish, but they preserve purity and interior simplicity.

~General Audience, March 18, 2015

Reflection: Sometimes we like children so much we think they're better than they are—we even call them "little angels." They are not little angels—they can be bad, too—but their simplicity and purity does reflect some of the beauty of heaven. We can get so complicated in the way we do things and look at life. Learning how to be simple like children, indeed, brings us closer to the angels.

September 29

How St. Michael Triumphs

Feast of Sts. Michael, Gabriel, and Raphael

CR

ST. MICHAEL THE ARCHANGEL … defends the People of God from their enemies and above all from the archenemy par excellence, the devil. And St. Michael triumphs because in him it is God who acts.

~Address, Blessing of the Statue of
St. Michael, Vatican Gardens, July 5, 2013

Reflection: St. Michael is the great archangel who defends us in battle. We may have to battle for many things in this life, but let's not forget that the battle that matters most is the one we fight against the devil—because nothing else can separate us from God.

St. Michael can defend us because God acts in him. Whenever we allow God to act in us, we win.

St. Michael, defend us in battle—and help us to choose our battles wisely!

September 30

He Won't Stop Knocking

☙

JESUS KEEPS KNOCKING ON OUR DOORS, the doors of our lives. He doesn't do this by magic, with special effects, with flashing lights and fireworks.

Jesus keeps knocking on our door in the faces of our brothers and sisters, in the faces of our neighbors, in the faces of those at our side.

~Address to the Homeless, St. Patrick Parish,
Washington, D.C., September 24, 2015

Reflection: In many places, kids will play a game called "ring and run"—you ring a doorbell and then run while someone is coming to answer it. My kids used to do this at our own front door when they were little. It's funny because it's annoying—we all know that doorbells don't ring themselves, there is no magic involved.

Sometimes, it seems as if we think that God is magic rather than mystery: his ways are unknown and often mysterious to us, but he works through real people and real events. He keeps knocking, but we have to get up and answer the door.

October 1

Small, Quiet Signs

Feast of St. Thérèse of Lisieux

ର

LIKE HAPPINESS, HOLINESS IS ALWAYS TIED TO LITTLE GESTURES. "Whoever gives you a cup of water in my name will not go unrewarded," says Jesus (cf. Mk 9:41). These little gestures are those we learn at home, in the family; they get lost amid all the other things we do, yet they do make each day different.

They are the quiet things done by mothers and grandmothers, by fathers and grandfathers, by children, by brothers and sisters. They are little signs of tenderness, affection and compassion. Like the warm supper we look forward to at night, the early lunch awaiting someone who gets up early to go to work. [Home] gestures. Like a blessing before we go to bed, or a hug after we return from a hard day's work. Love is shown by little things, by attention to small daily signs which make us feel at home.

~Homily, Closing Mass, World Meeting of Families,
Philadelphia, September 27, 2015

Reflection: The "butterfly effect" refers to ways that small changes in an environment can lead to major transformations in that environment over time. Something that seems very small can have a huge impact later on.

St. Thérèse of Lisieux is known and loved by many as a great saint and doctor of the Church—she's even a patron of the missions even though she never left France and died at age twenty-four. But when she was sick and dying, some of the sisters in her convent wondered what anyone was going to say about her when she died—they hadn't seen much that they thought was remarkable or impressive.

Sometimes, little things seem smaller than they really are—to ourselves and to others. Over time, they have a butterfly effect. St. Thérèse called her approach the "little way"—we can follow that way knowing it leads to much greater things, and much greater love.

October 2

God's Ambassador

Feast of the Guardian Angels

ଔ

[OUR GUARDIAN ANGEL] IS ALWAYS WITH US, and this is a reality: he is like an ambassador of God with us.... He advises us, accompanies us, walks with us in the name of God....

God sends us the angel ... to free us, to lead us away from fear, to lead us away from misfortune. [And] he asks only that we listen to him, respect him.

~Homily, *Domus Sanctae Marthae*,
October 2, 2015

Reflection: Sometimes we see images of people with an angel on one shoulder and a devil on the other. The devil is usually trying to convince the person to do something "fun," while the angel wants them to do something good.

But that's not how it is. Yes, the devil sometimes tempts us to do bad things that we think will be fun, but he mostly brings fear and darkness into our lives—he gets us to do bad things, thinking they'll be fun, and then takes away the fun.

Our guardian angel wants to lead us away from that. Listen and watch; you'll see who will show you a better time.

October 3

Learning to Give

CR

I LIKE TO ASK CHILDREN, "If you have two sweets and you see a friend, what do you do?" Most frequently they reply, "I give them one." That is the general response. "And what do you do if you have only one sweet and you see your friend coming?"

Here they hesitate. And the responses vary between, "I give it to him," "I share it" to "I put it back into my pocket." The child who learns is the one who knows how to be generous to others.

~Address, Meeting with Civic Leaders,
Quito, Ecuador, July 7, 2015

Reflection: Sometimes, I give away things that I don't use very much to friends or family members. Then, when I see someone else using them, I want them back! But I know I don't—and didn't— need them. It can be easy to second-guess our decision to share or to give things to others.

Jesus said that when you give alms, you shouldn't let your right hand know what your left hand is doing. Often, if we spend too much time thinking about it, we don't do it; it's easy to find selfish reasons not to! Learning to be generous is learning not to think so hard about sharing, realizing that my generosity benefits me first of all, by opening my heart.

Just give!

October 4

Peace in Trials

CR

WHATEVER DIFFICULTIES AND TRIALS YOU FACE, I ask you … to be at peace and to respond to them as Christ did: He thanked the Father, took up his cross, and looked forward!

~Homily, Vespers, New York City,
September 25, 2015

Reflection: When we go through difficult times, we often try to understand *why*: what we did wrong, and how we can fix it. And if we can't fix it this time, how can we avoid the problem in the future.

This tendency is helpful in many ways. But sometimes it hurts us: it distracts us from the fact that God is allowing us to pass through these circumstances right now, whatever caused them. Even if things are "our fault," he loves us, he loves us *right now*. We can be at peace knowing that.

Father, give us the grace of your Son to thank you in all situations, to take up our crosses and look forward.

October 5

Where True Happiness Can Be Found

ଔ

[JESUS] DOES NOT TRICK YOU. Because he knows that happiness, true happiness, the happiness which can fill our hearts, is not found in designer clothing, or expensive brand-name shoes.

He knows that real happiness is found in drawing near to others, learning how to weep with those who weep, being close to those who are feeling low or in trouble, giving them a shoulder to cry on, a hug.

~Address, Meeting with Young People,
Asunción, Paraguay, July 12, 2015

Reflection: We live in a world that focuses on images of what makes people happy, instead of what really *does* make us happy. So, when we think of happiness, we think of money, power, and fame—and forget how miserable many rich, powerful celebrities are.

We forget very easily that we were made to give of ourselves; that our very own satisfaction consists in giving our lives. Our *own* happiness is in loving and being loved. Can I let go of my images of false happiness and recognize what really brings joy?

October 6

He Extends His Hand

CR

[JESUS] MADE HIMSELF OUR COMPANION along the way. Not only does he encourage us he also accompanies us; he is at our side, and he extends a friendly hand to us.

~Address to Students, Havana, Cuba,
September 20, 2015

Reflection: It's an uncomfortable moment when we try to shake someone's hand and they ignore ours. It's embarrassing, but it's cruel if people do it deliberately to someone who cares for them.

In becoming man, God accompanies us in everything we do: his hand is ready and extended. Will we reach out and take his hand—or leave him hanging?

October 7

Wherever Jesus Is, There Is Joy

CR

WHEREVER THERE ARE DREAMS, wherever there is joy, Jesus is always present. Always. But who is it that sows sadness, that sows mistrust, envy, evil desires? What is his name? The devil.

The devil always sows sadness, because he doesn't want us to be happy; he doesn't want us to dream.

Wherever there is joy, Jesus is always present, because Jesus is joy, and he wants to help us to feel that joy every day of our lives.

~Address, Meeting with Immigrant Families,
Harlem, New York, September 25, 2015

Reflection: In the Garden of Eden, there was no mistrust before the serpent came along. It was the devil that brought mistrust, envy, and death into the world.

How does the devil ruin our joy? He does it by confusing us like the serpent did—by making us think there are things better than the life, love, and joy God wants for us. He distracts us and makes us waste our time chasing forms of happiness that never come.

God always wants to give us his joy in the present: here and now. Jesus came so that we could recover what we had lost through sin.

October 8

Salvation Freely Given

CR

THE STRUGGLE TO CONTROL SALVATION—only those who do these things are saved—did not end with Jesus and Paul.... It can be good for us to ask ourselves today: Do I believe that the Lord saved me freely? Do I believe that I do not deserve salvation?

And if I do merit something, do I believe it is through Jesus Christ and what he has done for me? It is a good question: Do I believe in the gratuitousness of salvation?

And, finally, do I believe that the only answer is love, the commandment of love, which Jesus says summarizes all the law and the teachings of all the prophets?

~Homily, *Domus Sanctae Marthae*,
October 15, 2015

Reflection: If someone opens the door for me, I say thank you. No one owes it to me to open the door; people open the door out of their generosity and goodness, not because they see that I'm a good person and deserve it.

Yet, somehow, religious people can start thinking that somehow God owes it to us to open his door. Do I do things because I think they'll force God to open the door, or do I do them because I want to learn his amazing way of being?

The way of wonder, wonder at God's generosity and goodness, is much more interesting—and more true—than thinking we're going to "make" him let us into heaven.

October 9
Together with Christ

രു

ONLY TOGETHER WITH JESUS, praying to him and following him, do we find clarity of vision and strength to go forward. He loves us definitively, he has chosen us definitively, he gave himself to each of us definitively.

He is our defender and big brother, and will be our only judge. How beautiful it is to be able to face life's ups and downs in Jesus' company, to have his Person and his message with us!

~Address, Meeting with Young People,
Castelpetroso, Italy, July 5, 2014

Reflection: The Trinity is a great mystery. But one of the things it reveals is that there is a community within the unity of God himself. He is never alone, and doesn't leave us alone, either!

God wants us to realize that he is always with us, and that his companionship is itself the greatest gift he gives us. He is always with us on the road of life.

October 10

United in Love

ભ

JESUS PRAYS THAT WE WILL ALL BECOME PART of a great family in which God is our Father, in which all of us are brothers and sisters. No one is excluded; and this is not about having the same tastes, the same concerns, the same gifts. We are brothers and sisters because God created us out of love and destined us, purely of his own initiative, to be his sons and daughters (cf. Eph 1:5).

~Homily, Mass, Quito, Ecuador, July 7, 2015

Reflection: St. Paul talks about our being "adopted sons" of God. When a family adopts a child, they don't have a child because it just "happened," they have a child because they wanted to share their love with someone; their love is stronger than biology.

We are all God's children by adoption. We may be very different in many ways, but we are united by his love. He loved us first, and nothing is stronger than that bond.

October 11

Our Daily Gospel

☙

I'LL ASK YOU A QUESTION, but I don't want you to answer: How many of you read a passage of the Gospel every day? How many of you, perhaps, rush to finish work so you don't miss a TV program....

To have the Gospel in your hands, to have the Gospel on your bedside table, to have the Gospel in your pocket, to open it and read the Word of Jesus: this is how the kingdom of God comes.

Contact with the Word of God draws us near to the kingdom of God. Consider this: a small Gospel always at hand, ready to open when the opportunity arises, ready to read what Jesus says. Jesus is there.

~Homily, Mass, Caserta, Italy, July 26, 2014

Reflection: People's lives are so busy it's easy to feel like there is no time to do things. But we always find time for the things we really love.

We can make it easier to give space to God and his word by having a small book of the Gospels or Bible handy and reading it often. When we are eating our breakfast, waiting for someone, or have a couple of minutes to spare, we can read our pocket Bible before we turn to an electronic device or the TV.

October 12

Grateful for All Those Who Defend Human Dignity

CB

I ... THANK ALL THOSE, OF WHATEVER RELIGION, who have sought to serve God, the God of peace, by building cities of brotherly love, by caring for our neighbors in need, by defending the dignity of God's gift, the gift of life in all its stages, and by defending the cause of the poor and the immigrant.

All too often, those most in need of our help, everywhere, are unable to be heard. You are their voice.

~Address, Meeting for Religious Liberty,
Philadelphia, September 26, 2015

Reflection: In Paul's Letter to the Romans, he states that God shows no partiality, and notes that both those who had the law and those who didn't disobeyed it, yet Jesus came for all, that they all might be saved.

There are many people in our cities and societies who are not Christian, or even religious, but recognize what is good and build on it. God's grace passes mysteriously through them as well. Let us look attentively at everything and retain what is good. And let us give thanks for those who have provided for so many in their need!

October 13

Cherishing Freedom

ભ

LET US PRESERVE FREEDOM. Let us cherish freedom. Freedom of conscience, religious freedom, the freedom of each person, each family, each people, which is what gives rise to rights.

May this country and each of you be renewed in gratitude for the many blessings and freedoms that you enjoy. And may you defend these rights, especially your religious freedom, for it has been given to you by God himself.

~Address, Meeting for Religious Liberty,
Philadelphia, September 26, 2015

Reflection: Freedom is a precious gift: everyone likes to be and to feel free. But we love freedom especially because it is a reflection of God. God could have made us differently. He could have made us so that we just automatically did everything he wanted and everything he knew was good.

But that's not what he wanted. He didn't want the human race forced into doing his bidding, like robots or slaves. He wanted people who could freely choose to love him, despite the challenges and difficulties. Our very ability to love him depends on our freedom: true love is free.

May we embrace and defend freedom, knowing what is at stake.

October 14

Society Rises on the Foundation of the Family

☙

FAMILY LIFE IS SOMETHING WORTHWHILE, and ... a society grows
stronger and better, it grows in beauty and it grows in truth, when
it rises on the foundation of the family.

~Address, Prayer Vigil, Philadelphia,
September 26, 2015

Reflection: When houses are strong and stable, they provide
shelter and, often, much more for the people who live in them.
That's why we build them. When you want to change the house
in some significant way, an architect will need to confirm that the
changes will not compromise its structural integrity. This may mean
reviewing the foundation to make sure it can bear any changes or
additions to the house.

Today, we often fail to see that the family is the true foundation
of society, but that's what the family is. It came before society; the
family is part of nature itself, and the more we cultivate a strong
family life, the more we build a better and happier society.

October 15

What Do You Want, Lord?

☙

THIS IS THE PRAYER THAT A YOUNG PERSON should make: "Lord what do you want from me?"

~Address, Meeting with Asian Youth,
Dangjin, South Korea, August 15, 2014

Reflection: There is a famous prayer and poem that has also been set to music and is attributed to St. Teresa of Ávila. "I am yours," she says. "What do you want me to do?"

We are his. What does God want from us—from *me*?

It is important for all of us to ask this question, but most importantly for young people, because so much depends on asking the right questions early. Life is so much more beautiful and true if we listen to the Lord when we are first starting down life's path.

October 16

Letting Go of the Favorite

CR

I REMEMBER ONCE HOW MY MOTHER was asked which of her five children—we are five brothers—did she love the most. And she said: It is like the fingers on my hand. If I prick one of them, then it is as if the others are pricked also. A mother loves her children as they are. And in the family, children are loved as they are. None are rejected.

~Homily, Mass for Families,
Guayaquil, Ecuador, July 6, 2015

Reflection: Children often want to know who is the "favorite"—we are always comparing ourselves to everyone else. We can't believe that we really are all loved just as we are, and so we need to prove that we are somehow superior. But the struggle to be superior—to be the favorite—takes a lot out of us and poisons the way we treat one another.

It can be so hard to believe that we really are all loved as we are—but life is so much better when we realize it's true, and that we can stop fighting to be on top!

October 17

The Family: God's Most Beautiful Creation

ॐ

THE MOST BEAUTIFUL THING GOD MADE—so the Bible tells us—was the family. He created man and woman. And he gave them everything. He entrusted the world to them: "Grow, multiply, cultivate the earth, make it bear fruit, let it grow."

All the love he put into that marvelous creation he entrusted to a family.

~Address, Prayer Vigil, Philadelphia,
September 26, 2015

Reflection: If you've ever owned a healthy fruit tree, you know it produces much more fruit than you know what to do with. You need to invite people over to pick and share the harvest if you don't want it to just rot away on the ground.

When we hear the creation story, it's clear that everything God made was good. And all of this good stuff was given to a man and woman to enjoy and make use of! It was obviously *way* more than they needed—and that was part of his plan. He wanted that extreme generosity to be part of their understanding of themselves and their own families.

God knew that they would make mistakes, but he also gave it all to them, trusting that, made in his image, they would bring the same awareness of God's generosity into their own families.

Just as the first family was given more than they could possibly need, God bets on our families and us, that just as he has given us above and beyond what we need, we will learn to give in the same way to each other.

October 18

Great Faith Through Prayer

CR

THERE MUST NEVER BE A LACK OF PRAYER FOR THE SICK.... Let us consider the Gospel episode of the Canaanite woman (cf. Mt 15:21-28). She is a pagan woman. She is not of the People of Israel, but a pagan who implores Jesus to heal her daughter. To test her faith, Jesus at first responds harshly: "I cannot, I must think first of the sheep of Israel."

The woman does not give up—when a mother asks for help for her infant, she never gives up; we all know that mothers fight for their children—and she replies, "Even dogs are given something when their masters have eaten," as if to say, "At least treat me like a dog!" Thus Jesus says to her: "Woman, great is your faith! Be it done for you as you desire" (v. 28).

~General Audience, June 10, 2015

Reflection: Sometimes schools or companies or other groups do "trust exercises"—such as making people fall backward into other people's arms in order to build team spirit and trust amongst their students or employees. Our natural instinct is to be afraid; we have to learn to trust that there are people who really will catch us.

When people are sick or suffering for a long time, it's hard for us to understand what God is doing and what he wants from us and for us. What he wants most is that we learn to trust. And the first and best way of doing that is not to give up praying.

October 19

Drawing Upon His Saving Grace

CR

TO TOUCH JESUS IS TO DRAW FROM HIM the grace that saves. It saves us, it saves our spiritual life, it saves us from so many problems.

~Angelus, June 18, 2015

Reflection: There are a number of passages in the Gospels where people who need healing try to find a way to touch Jesus: his healing power passes through him almost like electricity.

How do we touch him? There are many ways, but we can start by finding him in the sacraments, by reaching out for him in confession and in Communion, and by reaching out to people we know to be holy. He longs to heal us.

October 20

Knocking on the Door of Our Hearts

ભ્

GOD ALWAYS KNOCKS ON THE DOORS OF OUR HEARTS. He likes to do that. He goes out from within.

But do you know what he likes best of all? To knock on the doors of families. And to see families which are united, families which love, families which bring up their children, educating them and helping them to grow, families which build a society of goodness, truth, and beauty.

~Address, Prayer Vigil, Philadelphia,
September 26, 2015

Reflection: Heaven is frequently compared to a great feast in the Bible. God likes to be alone with us, but the greatest happiness is compared to a wonderful party where we can be together with all the people we love most, having an amazing time.

Big families often feel like their lives are crazy and hectic—but many people enjoy being with them anyway, because their lives feel like a party. A happy family is a party waiting to happen. When God knocks on our door, he's looking to find that—and to bring that truth home.

October 21

Serving Our Siblings in the Lord

☙

CHRISTIANS ... GO TO MEET THE POOR AND THE WEAK, not to obey a ... program, but because the word and the example of the Lord tell us that we are all brothers and sisters.

~General Audience, February 18, 2015

Reflection: Mother Teresa used to go out to the poor and suffering every day. But she didn't go to serve them just because she was nice or felt sorry for them. She ministered to them and cared for them because she saw the face of Jesus in them.

When it seems too hard to care for the weak and poor, or we just don't feel like it, let's ask Christ to show us his face in them!

October 22

Only Love Resolves Difficulties

CR

CHILDREN ARE HARD WORK. When we were children, we were hard work. Sometimes, back home I see some of my staff who come to work with rings under their eyes. They have a one- or two-month-old baby. And I ask them, "Didn't you get any sleep?" And they say, "No, the baby cried all night."

In families, there are difficulties, but those difficulties are resolved by love. Hatred doesn't resolve any difficulty. Divided hearts do not resolve difficulties. Only love is capable of resolving difficulty. Love is a celebration, love is joy, love is perseverance.

~Address, Prayer Vigil, Philadelphia,
September 26, 2015

Reflection: Mother Teresa once said, "I have found the paradox, that if you love until it hurts, there can be no more hurt, only more love." There may be no more hurt—but there is still more work, as Mother Teresa certainly knew well! Newborn babies especially test many parents this way. As hard as it is to function without sleep, parents do it out of love for their children.

Sometimes we get hurt in our families because we think family members are *trying* to hurt us and don't care how they make our lives difficult. But let's take a lesson from newborn babies: that usually, it's just how they are—they don't know any better, they hurt us by accident or because of their own weakness.

We can learn to resent them less when we understand this. We have to stay awake, and work, but that work brings us more—and greater—love.

October 23

God's Instruments

೧೩

YOU, DADS AND MOMS, HAVE THIS SPARK OF GOD which you give to your children, you are an instrument of God's love, and this is beautiful, beautiful, beautiful!

~General Audience, October 14, 2015

Reflection: What does it mean to be an instrument of God's love?

Usually, when we think of being an instrument, it feels like something less important, it's like being used by someone. But imagine the way a great musician plays a violin. The musician is gifted, but no one can hear his music without the violin. There is no real beauty without the instrument!

We have the ability to be God's instruments in this. We are the means to his most beautiful music in the world. *Us.*

October 24

Ending the Day in Peace

ℭℜ

IN THE FAMILY, SOMETIMES THERE IS FIGHTING. The husband argues with the wife; they get upset with each other, or children get upset with their parents.

May I offer a bit of advice: never end the day without making peace in the family. In the family the day cannot end in fighting.

~Address, Prayer Vigil, Philadelphia,
September 26, 2015

Reflection: Researchers have found that, when it comes to memories, there are a few things that stick in people's heads much more than anything else: how something began, the best and worst moments, and how it ended. It's true with fighting and arguments, too—whether we fight a little or a lot.

Whether it's a big fight or just a really bad day, we can't change everything, but we can choose how we end things. We can apologize. We can say "I love you" to someone we've hurt. And if we're still too angry or upset to do those things, we can still pray that the Lord will change our own hearts.

October 25

Detachment from Possessions

ଔ

THE THIRST OF ATTACHMENT TO POSSESSIONS never ends. If your heart is attached to possessions—when you have many—you want more. And this is the god of a person attached to possessions. [Jesus] explains the way to salvation, the Beatitudes, the first is poverty of spirit, that is, "don't be attached to possessions."

~Homily, *Domus Sanctae Marthae*,
October 19, 2015

Reflection: "What do you seek?" is the first question that Jesus asks his first disciples. He asks us the same question.

In the end, we have to decide what we really want: the kingdom—or the king himself? We can only choose one, and only one of them lasts.

October 26

Making Others' Lives Easier

◌

LIFE IS NOT EASY FOR MANY YOUNG PEOPLE. And I want you to understand this, and I want you to keep it always in mind: "If my life is relatively easy, there are other young men and women whose lives are not relatively easy."

What is more, desperation drives them to crime, drives them to get involved in corruption. To those young people, we want to say that we are close to them, we want to lend them a helping hand, we want to support them, with solidarity, love, and hope.

~Address, Meeting with Young People,
Asunción, Paraguay, July 12, 2015

Reflection: I once saw a documentary about a community of women with AIDS in Nairobi. Many of them didn't think life was worth living—they had no reason to live, no reason to hope, given their poverty and illness.

But after meeting some Christians who looked at them with love and treated them with compassion, they started looking at life differently; they started taking their medicine and dancing in their free time.

When Hurricane Katrina hit New Orleans, some of these same women were moved with compassion to work extra jobs in order to send money to those suffering from the storm's effects. Many other richer, healthier people did much less. These women knew what it meant to give and to receive—and that moved them to give everything they had, and more.

Even those of us with easy lives have our hardships. Let us pray that our hardships will soften our hearts and give us greater compassion, in word and deed. We are all one in Christ—let's not forget that!

October 27

It Is Not Good to Be Alone

ᏬᎡ

GOD ... FROM THE VERY BEGINNING OF CREATION, SAID, "It is not good for man to be alone" (Gn 2:18). We can add: it is not good for woman to be alone, it is not good for children, the elderly, or the young to be alone. It is not good....

From time immemorial, in the depths of our heart, we have heard those powerful words: it is not good for you to be alone. The family is the great blessing, the great gift of this "God with us," who did not want to abandon us to the solitude of a life without others, without challenges, without a home.

~Address, Prayer Vigil, Philadelphia,
September 26, 2015

Reflection: God is never alone. It was not good for man to be alone, either, which is why God made man and woman: united in difference, in God's image. This is the beauty of the family. It reflects God's image and gives us a fuller chance to learn to live like him.

October 28

God Hears Their Cry

ဢ

EVERY CHILD WHO IS MARGINALIZED, abandoned, who lives on the street begging with every kind of trick, without schooling, without medical care, is a cry that rises up to God.

~General Audience, April 8, 2015

Reflection: We often say that actions speak louder than words. Sometimes, actions pray louder than words. This can be true of our lack of action as well: God hears the prayer of the needy and sad. Do we?

October 29
It's the Lord's Call

ॐ

WHEN THE LORD CALLS, he always does so for the good of others, whether it is through the religious life ... or as a layperson, as the father or mother of a family. The goal is the same: to worship God and to do good to others....

I once asked it myself: What path should I choose? But you do not have to choose any path! The Lord must choose it! Jesus has chosen it! You have to listen to him and ask: Lord, what should I do?

~Address, Meeting with Asian Youth,
Dangjin, South Korea, August 15, 2014

Reflection: It's hard for us to remember what it means, that we are created by God! We tend to think so many things are up to us, so many decisions to be made—and they often feel heavy. We can spend so much time spinning our wheels, figuring out what to do.

But God knows us better than we know ourselves; I don't need to choose a path—I need to follow one. The Lord's voice is usually a still, small one; I can't hear it unless I pay attention.

Can I listen to where he's leading me now?

October 30

Staking Everything on Love

ℭℛ

LET US HELP ONE ANOTHER to make it possible to "stake everything on love." Let us help one another during times of difficulty and lighten each other's burdens.

Let us support one another. Let us be families which are a support for other families.

~Address, Prayer Vigil, Philadelphia,
September 26, 2015

Reflection: Many times, our lives can seem boring, flat, or difficult. But when we pay attention and speak honestly to the people around us, we discover how many challenges they face as well!

Often we stop feeling sorry for ourselves when we reach out to another person who is suffering or needy. When we do this, it's like we feel our hearts expand, and we breathe again. Can we lighten someone else's burden?

October 31

The Family Is No Place for Just "Me, Myself, and I"

ଔ

THE FAMILY IS A SCHOOL OF HUMANITY, a school which teaches us to open our hearts to others' needs, to be attentive to their lives.

When we live together ... as a family, we keep our little ways of being selfish in check—they will always be there, because each of us has a touch of selfishness—but when there is no family life, what results are those "me, myself and I" personalities who are completely self-centered and lacking any sense of solidarity, fraternity, cooperation, love, and fraternal disagreements. They don't have it.

~Address, Meeting with Families,
Santiago, Cuba, September 22, 2015

Reflection: Many people manage to avoid their little bad habits when others are around—and they may not even realize it unless they get caught on video when they're alone and don't think anyone else can see them.

The same is true with bigger things as well. We learn to curb some of our selfishness in family life. Family life naturally builds awareness and a concern for others. We are all naturally selfish—and the family is a natural antidote to that.

November 1

Surrounded by a Cloud of Witnesses

Feast of All Saints

☙

ON THIS JOURNEY WE ARE NOT ALONE. We help one another by our example and by our prayers. We are surrounded by a cloud of witnesses (cf. Heb 12:1)....That cloud of witnesses!

May we press forward with the help and cooperation of all; for the Lord wants to use us to make his light reach to every corner of our world. Go forward, sing and walk.

~Address, Meeting with Clergy, Santa Cruz
de la Sierra, Bolivia, July 9, 2015

Reflection: When we look up at the sky, clouds seem like a pretty part of the background. But when a storm rolls in, we realize how powerful those clouds are!

Sometimes, we can think that way about the Church or the saints—like they're just a pretty part of our life's background. Instead, that cloud of witnesses, like clouds themselves, is powerful indeed. The Church's people—both living and dead—are a powerful witness, and they help us press on in our journey.

November 2

Hope Does Not Disappoint

All Souls' Day

೫

AFTER JESUS BROUGHT THE YOUNG MAN, the only son of a widow, back to life [cf. Lk 7:11-15], the Gospel says: "Jesus gave him back to his mother." And this is our hope!

All our loved ones who are gone, the Lord will give them back to us, and we will be together with them. This hope does not disappoint!

Let us remember well this action of Jesus: "And Jesus gave him back to his mother," thus the Lord will do with all our loved ones in the family … when death will be definitively conquered in us. It was conquered by Jesus' cross.

~General Audience, June 17, 2015

Reflection: Nothing—and no one—is lost with Christ. This is our great reason for hope, and a key reason that Jesus' life, death, and resurrection are called good news for the world. Even when we lose the people dearest to us, let us not lose hope.

Lord, help me to hope in you!

November 3

Jesus Is the Bread of Life for Families

CR

THE EUCHARIST IS THE MEAL OF JESUS' FAMILY, in which the world over gathers to hear his word and to be fed by his body.

Jesus is the Bread of Life for our families. He wants to be ever present, nourishing us by his love, sustaining us in faith, helping us to walk in hope, so that in every situation we can experience the true Bread of Heaven.

~Address, Meeting with Families,
Santiago, Cuba, September 22, 2015

Reflection: One of the first things a mother does for a newborn child is to feed her. When we eat food, that food is broken down by our digestive system and its components are transported throughout our bodies.

Jesus wants to be with us so badly that he offered his body to us on the cross and every time Mass is celebrated throughout the world. He wants to feed us, nourish us, live within us. Literally.

November 4

Pursuing Purity of Heart

 barC

WE NEED TO SHOW A HEALTHY CONCERN for creation, for the purity of our air, water, and food, but how much more do we need to protect the purity of what is most precious of all: *our heart and our relationships.*

~Message for the Thirtieth World Youth Day, 2015

Reflection: Everyone likes to go to beautiful beaches: beaches where the sand is clean and the water—some of us can go on and on about the water—is the perfect shade of turquoise, so clear you can see all the fish swimming in it. We know what pure water looks like: it's amazing.

It's a little harder to describe the beauty of pure hearts and relationships, but it's even more beautiful. When someone loves us without strings attached, when someone's heart is pure, it is a magnificent thing. We want to be around people like that, even if we don't know quite why.

That purity is something we need to cultivate and defend more than anything, because without it, our whole world starts to look murky and dark, our entire lives get polluted.

November 5

Saying No to Discouragement

ભ

Never yield to discouragement, do not lose trust, do not allow your hope to be extinguished.

Situations can change; people can change. Be the first to seek to bring good, do not grow accustomed to evil, but defeat it with good.

~Address, Visit to Varginha, Rio de Janeiro,
Brazil, July 25, 2013

Reflection: Nothing lasts, they say. And it's true in the natural order of things: children grow up, neighborhoods change, people move away. Thinking about this in relation to things and people we love may make us sad.

But it's also true of the things we don't like and which challenge us. Things are constantly in motion—even those hard things (and people!) are in the process of transformation.

There is another saying: "Be patient: God's not finished with me yet!" He's not finished with any of us. Let's be patient and trust.

November 6

Coming Together to Lead

଼

TODAY WE SEE THAT THE WORLD IS being destroyed by war, because people are incapable of sitting down and talking. "Good, let's negotiate. What can we do together? Where are we going to draw the line? But let's not kill any more people."

Where there is division, there is death: the death of the soul, since we are killing our ability to come together.

~Address to Students, Havana, Cuba,
September 20, 2015

Reflection: Many people in the world talk about being leaders, and how important it is to lead. If someone leads, then someone else must be following, because otherwise the leader is just a single, opinionated individual.

Sometimes, it's difficult to sit down and talk to someone who doesn't agree with us, because we think they should just agree with us and do what we say. But true leadership consists in gaining real followers. Otherwise, we destroy both the world we live in and lose our own souls in the name of lesser things.

November 7

Life Is Yours!

❦

Do not be afraid, do not let your hope be stolen. Life is yours! It's yours to make flourish, to bear fruit for everyone.
~Address, Phone Call to Scouts, August 10, 2014

Reflection: Life is a promise. Sometimes, in moments of difficulty, we doubt that promise. But whatever challenges or trials come our way, God never reneges on his promise. Never: He is with us, always.

Take the risk of taking him at his word—you will not be disappointed!

November 8

Unity Is a Gift

☙

UNITY IS OFTEN CONFUSED with uniformity; with actions, feelings, and words which are all identical. This is not unity; it is conformity. It kills the life of the Spirit; it kills the charisms which God has bestowed for the good of his people.

Unity is threatened whenever we try to turn others into our own image and likeness. Unity is a gift, not something to be imposed by force or by decree.

~Homily, Vespers, Havana, Cuba,
September 20, 2015

Reflection: We often think of unity as sameness. But the profoundest unity is found in diversity, diversity in the service of the something greater. Our body is made up of very different parts—but its great unity is a result of working for the same purposes, to keep us alive and working.

When we look at others, recognizing that they have the same Father in heaven and that they are made for heaven as we are, we discover a unity with them we never dreamed of. A unity that connects us to one another, despite our differences, and which never forces us to be too much alike.

Freedom and unity come from the same source.

November 9

Moving on from Mistakes

CR

ALL OF US HAVE MADE MISTAKES and been caught up in misunderstandings, a thousand of them. Happy, then, are those who can help others when they make mistakes, when they experience misunderstandings. They are true friends, they do not give up on anyone.
~Address, Meeting with Young People,
Asunción, Paraguay, July 12, 2015

Reflection: Life gets so complicated sometimes! So many small misunderstandings and little problems that then become big problems.

I know many people who aren't speaking to friends or family members over incidents that didn't start as big issues. Other people do thoughtless and unkind things. But so do we!

God doesn't ask us to do anything he hasn't already done for us; he wants to give us the strength to put up with our annoying friends and family. But will we accept his gift of strength?

November 10

His Forgiveness Never Ends

ೞ

GOD NEVER TIRES OF FORGIVING. And this is true! So great is his love, which is always near us. It is we who tire of asking for forgiveness, but he always forgives, every time we ask him to.

~Address, Meeting with Young People,
Castelpetroso, Italy, July 5, 2014

Reflection: We (humans) get tired of forgiving. Sometimes we say to our friends or family, "If you're really sorry, you'll change—you'll stop doing X or Y!" And it's true that wanting to change is a sign of being truly sorry.

But change is also hard, and it can take a long time. God knows this—and he forgives even when we wouldn't. We need to realize that we are the ones who lose patience—not him. It's up to us to ask for forgiveness—it's so simple! He never gets tired of forgiving. Just ask!

November 11

Hope for Young and Old Alike

☙

WHERE THERE IS NO HONOR FOR [THE ELDERLY], there is no future for the young.

~General Audience, March 4, 2015

Reflection: In our world, everyone wants to stay young. It's hard to find people who truly value the elderly. We also see many children and young people who feel lost, depressed, and alienated.

It doesn't seem like there is much of a connection, but children can see what is in store for them when they get older, and it makes it harder for them to hope for a future. When we honor the elderly among us, we pave the way for a better life for everyone.

Lord, help us to treat young and old with dignity and inspire hope in all we meet.

November 12

God Is a Master

ରୁ

GOD IS A MASTER at finding a way to resolve things.
~In-flight Press Conference, September 27, 2015

Reflection: Sometimes, in life, we look at things and think there's no answer, there's no solution, that things are just too far gone. This can happen with big things: our careers, our families, or with little ones, like our children's over-flowing toy box, the yard, or the laundry situation.

Let's remember again that we worship a God who died a bloody, naked, excruciatingly painful death, and then *rose again*. He can resolve whatever he wants, however impossible it is. What he asks of us is to believe: to trust that he can do it and remain certain of his love when he doesn't fix things the way we want.

November 13

Bridges Are Better Solutions

ଔ

WALLS ARE NEVER SOLUTIONS, but bridges always are.
~In-flight Press Conference, September 27, 2015

Reflection: Walls are great for supporting a house: they keep the weather outside and everything else inside. But they're not so good for communicating.

When people are difficult, or hard to understand, we often want to avoid them: we think about building a wall, or hiding behind one. But that wall doesn't prevent the person from existing. It just lets us ignore them.

A bridge, however, offers a point of connection to someplace. Sometimes, those connections are difficult and painful to make— bridges were built to pass over impassible things like rivers, and their construction can take a long time. But we can always build bridges, provided we decide we want to.

November 14

Be Courageous: Have Hope

℧

COURAGE AND HOPE ARE QUALITIES that everyone has, but they are most befitting in young people: courage and hope. The future is surely in the hands of God.... This does not mean denying difficulties and problems, but seeing them, yes, as temporary....

Difficulties, crises, can, with God's help and the good will of all, be overcome, defeated, transformed.

~Address, Meeting with Young People,
Castelpetroso, Italy, July 5, 2014

Reflection: Courage and hope go together. When I trust in God and have hope that even the most difficult situations can be transformed, I gain the courage to face challenges in my life and in the world.

Lord, give the hope that makes us courageous!

November 15

Friendship of the Saints

⊗

THE SAINTS ARE OUR FRIENDS AND MODELS. They no longer play on our field, but we continue to look to them in our efforts to play our best game.

They show us that Jesus is no con artist; he offers us genuine fulfillment. But above all, he offers us friendship, true friendship, the friendship we all need.

~Address, Meeting with Young People,
Asunción, Paraguay, July 12, 2015

Reflection: In the process of becoming a saint, one of the requirements is a verified miracle attributed to the candidate for sainthood. This is one of the Church's ways of testing, of making sure that a holy person is truly with God. The saint has died, but the miracle happens to a living person and reminds us of the connection between heaven and earth: we are never truly alone.

Friendship with Jesus—and with his friends, the saints—is always available to us.

What saint can I invoke in my desire to grow in friendship with Jesus? What saint can be my friend?

November 16

Never Forget

CR

NEVER FORGET, NEVER DENY YOUR ROOTS.... In the Book of Deuteronomy, how many times does God say to his People, "Do not forget, do not forget, do not forget." And Paul, to his beloved disciple Timothy, whom he ordained, says, "Remember your mother and grandmother."

~Address, Meeting with Clergy, Santa Cruz
de la Sierra, Bolivia, July 9, 2015

Reflection: When we think about the idea of remembering, we think of it as being related to the past—which it is. But remembering matters because it's also about the present.

More than one movie or television show has a main character who has lost his memory. Without memory, he doesn't know who he is. If we forget our roots, if we forget the faces of the people who have raised us and loved us and shown us God, we lose our own identity.

When it feels like an effort to remember things or people from our past, let us remember that God reaches us through them—and that remembering things that matter to others teaches us to love both them and God better.

November 17

The Tenderness of God and Children

൦ൠ

THE TENDER AND MYSTERIOUS RELATIONSHIP of God with the soul of children should never be violated. It is a real relationship, which God wants and God safeguards.

Children are ready from birth to feel loved by God; they are ready for this. As soon as children are able to feel they are loved for themselves, they also feel that there is a God who loves children.

~General Audience, October 14, 2015

Reflection: Many people have a soft spot for children. Sometimes, people even think of them as angels. Little children aren't angels, but they have a purity of heart that brings them naturally to God and a tenderness that communicates love very directly.

Helping children feel loved by God, showing them how precious they are in his eyes is a great gift that will last them—and us—a lifetime.

November 18

Caring for All, Cradle to Grave

ભ

WE HAVE TO CARE IN A SPECIAL WAY for children and for grand-parents. Children and young people are the future; they are our strength; they are what keep us moving forward. They are the ones in whom we put our hope.

Grandparents are a family's memory. They are the ones who gave us the faith, they passed the faith on to us. Taking care of grandparents and taking care of children is the sign of love.

~Address, Prayer Vigil, Philadelphia,
September 26, 2015

Reflection: Watching a video in slow motion can be really funny—and revealing. You see all the movements people make and their facial reactions. When we slow down, in the way we often have to do with children and some grandparents, we get to see things differently. We see that what's truly valuable really matters to us, and recognize the value that these slower moving people bring to us.

They remind us that we cannot live the present moment well without memory and without hope. We need real people to remind us of this, which is one of many reasons for caring for our grandparents and children with special care and tenderness.

November 19

We're All Thirsting for Peace

CR

I BELIEVE THAT THE WORLD TODAY is thirsting for peace. There are wars, waves of migrants, people fleeing from conflicts, fleeing death, seeking life. I was very moved that today, in the Casa Santa Marta, I met one of the two Syrian refugee families being hosted in the Vatican, in St. Anne's Parish. You could see the pain on their faces.

~In-flight Greeting to Journalists,
September 19, 2015

Reflection: It's always hard to make room for new people in our lives, and it's easy to find excuses. Our houses are too small; our lives are too busy.

Let us remember that they host refugees at the Vatican. Not everyone is called to host refugees in their homes, but we are all asked to make room for other people in our lives and hearts—and even, sometimes, in our actual homes as well.

November 20

Our Family Is a Home

‹Ϡ›

WHENEVER WE COME TOGETHER as a family, we feel at home.

~Address, Meeting with Families,
Santiago, Cuba, September 22, 2015

Reflection: When we think of home, we think of a place, a place where we can be relaxed, be ourselves, let our hair down, and wear sweatpants if we want. Our family is a sort of mobile home in that sense: as people grow up and get older, we may move from one home to another.

But being with our family gives us an opportunity to be ourselves and be comforted. This is a great blessing for all of us.

November 21

We Need One Another

ભ

BECAUSE EVERYTHING IS RELATED, we need one another.
~Address, Meeting with Civic Leaders,
La Paz, Bolivia, July 8, 2015

Reflection: "No man is an island," the poet John Donne wrote. We are all connected to one another, in ways that we see and also in mysterious ways we don't.

When God made the world, he said that it was exceedingly good. He made us male and female because he didn't want us to be alone. We need one another: there is no shame in that, because it's the way God made us—and it's exceedingly good.

November 22

His Healing Gaze

ᚴ

ON A DAY LIKE ANY OTHER, as Matthew, the tax collector, was seated at his table, Jesus passed by, saw him, came up to him, and said, "Follow me." Matthew got up and followed him.

Jesus stopped; he did not quickly turn away. He looked at Matthew calmly, peacefully. He looked at him with eyes of mercy; he looked at him as no one had ever looked at him before.

And that look unlocked Matthew's heart; it set him free, it healed him, it gave him hope, a new life.

~Homily, Mass, Holguín, Cuba,
September 21, 2015

Reflection: Many people remember the first time they saw the person they fell in love with. They may not have noticed the person's eye color, but they noticed the way someone looked at them! Something about it was unforgettable; it changed their life.

Being looked at with love and understanding might seem like a small thing at first, but it's huge. Can we imagine how Jesus looked at Matthew? He didn't just see him, he loved him, too. Jesus wants to heal us the same way. Do we meet his gaze?

November 23

Letting God Throw Us a Party

CR

THE PRODIGAL SON, THE SON WHO LEFT HOME, spent all his money, everything he had, betrayed his father and his family, betrayed everything. At a certain moment, out of necessity, but full of shame, he decided to return. He thought about how he would ask for his father's forgiveness. [and] say lots of ... fine things.

But the Gospel tells us that the father saw his son coming from afar. Why did he see him? Because every day he used to go out onto the terrace to see if his son would return. The father embraced him: he did not let his son speak ... and he did not allow him to even ask for forgiveness.

Then he went off to organize a party. This is the party that God enjoys: whenever we return home, whenever we return to him. "But Father, I am a sinful man, a sinful woman ..."

All the better, he is waiting for you! All the better, and he will throw a party!

~Address, Meeting with Asian Youth,
Dangjin, South Korea, August 15, 2014

Reflection: In a way, our shame is a twisted sort of pride. We think, "I should never have done something like this," or, "It is beneath someone like me to act this way," etc.

It's good for us to have standards and expectations, but not when they get in the way!

What is sin? It is turning away from God. So what God wants most is for us to turn back, for us to turn around and look at *him*, not at our own sin or mistakes. Because life is much better in his house. Lord, let me return to you.

November 24

Making Room

༼ྀ

[JESUS] COMES TO SAVE THE WORLD. And this is the great mission of the family: to make room for Jesus who is coming, to welcome Jesus in the family, in each member—children, husband, wife, grandparents.... Jesus is there. Welcome him there.

~General Audience, December 17, 2014

Reflection: When someone we love is coming to our house to visit, we find a place for him or her to sleep even if we don't have a guest room. We move people around and find a way. When we say we can't find room, usually it's because we don't have room in our hearts.

Finding room always starts with our hearts. Are we willing to give up that space and let Jesus come in?

November 25

Not to Condemn

CR

THE LORD ASKS US ABOVE ALL *not to judge* and *not to condemn*. If anyone wishes to avoid God's judgment, he should not make himself the judge of his brother or sister.

~*Misericordiae Vultus*, Bull of Indiction
for the Year of Mercy, 14

Reflection: What does it mean not to judge? It is natural to evaluate and try to understand other people's behavior—and even decide sometimes that their actions are bad. But there is so much we don't know about their thoughts, their difficulties and sufferings!

Not judging means that we don't like or understand others sometimes, but that we are still rooting for them, even when they make mistakes, still caring for them and hoping that things turn around, looking for signs of hope.

November 26

Let No One Steal Your Hope

ଓ

YOU, DEAR YOUNG PEOPLE, let no one steal your hope! I've said it many times and I will repeat it once more: Don't let them steal your hope!

Adoring Jesus in your hearts and staying united with him you will know how to stand up to evil, to injustice, and to violence with the strength of goodness, honesty, and virtue.

~Homily, Mass, Calabria, Italy,
June 21, 2015

Reflection: People can steal something without your realizing it—pickpockets do this—or they can force you to give up what you have, such as your wallet, at gunpoint, but no one can take your hope if you don't let them.

Your hope doesn't come from you—it comes from God himself, and he can and will put himself right back where he was in your life, as long as you let him. There is no thief who can outsmart him, or bullet that can stop him.

November 27

Every Family Is a Light

CB

EVERY FAMILY IS ALWAYS A LIGHT, however faint, amid the darkness of this world.

~Homily, Vigil in Preparation for Synod of Bishops,
Rome, October 3, 2015

Reflection: You can't have a family without sacrifices. The sacrifice of having a child, the sacrifice of keeping promises, the sacrifice of being obedient even some of the time. Whatever wrong we do, we are still a light.

Lord, help us burn more brightly—and help us recognize and cultivate our light!

November 28

The Lord Goes Searching

 C҂

THE LORD GOES IN SEARCH OF US; to all of us he stretches out a helping hand.

~Address, Visit to Detainees, Philadelphia,
September 27, 2015

Reflection: If we lose one dollar, but still have ninety-nine, how long would we spend looking for the dollar? Not long, I think. Because that one dollar really isn't worth much compared to all we have—it wouldn't make sense to look for it.

But if it was a dollar signed by someone famous, then we would look for it. Because its value wouldn't be the money itself—it's something else.

In the Gospel, when Jesus talks about leaving the ninety-nine sheep to look for the one sheep that is lost, he is showing us that there is a value in the sheep and that its value is bigger than a piece of property—he *loves* the sheep. He loves us, even if we don't understand why.

He is always looking for us, always ready and waiting to offer us the help we need, even in moments where we feel lost and abandoned.

November 29

A Great Nation

ෆ

A NATION CAN BE CONSIDERED GREAT when it defends liberty as [Abraham] Lincoln did, when it fosters a culture which enables people to "dream" of full rights for all their brothers and sisters, as Martin Luther King sought to do; when it strives for justice and the cause of the oppressed, as Dorothy Day did by her tireless work, the fruit of a faith which becomes dialogue and sows peace in the contemplative style of Thomas Merton.

~Address, Joint Session of U.S. Congress,
September 24, 2015

Reflection: An author I've read talks about "holy discontent"— the unease, the discomfort we feel with something that continues to bother us, and which is often the Lord calling us to a greater purpose, asking us to do something about it.

President Lincoln was unwilling to compromise on slavery; Dorothy Day lived and worked among the poor in New York City; Martin Luther King Jr. gave his life in the quest for racial equality. These were the beginning of dreams for a greater and better world: greater and better because it allowed more room for love, more room for human thriving.

November 30

The Authority of Service

 C？

FOR THE DISCIPLES OF JESUS, yesterday, today, and always, the only authority is the authority of service, the only power is the power of the cross.

As the Master tells us: "You know that the rulers of the Gentiles lord it over them, and their great men exercise authority over them. It shall not be so among you; but whoever would be great among you must be your servant, and whoever would be first among you must be your slave" (Mt 20:25-27).

~Address, Synod of the Chaldean Church,
Rome, October 17, 2015

Reflection: We often think those who serve are beneath those they are serving, because if you're in charge, you're the one telling people what to do. But if you have ever served, you know it's not that easy: to serve, you have to be well suited to your work; you have to learn to do it right.

No master keeps a servant who cannot do his job. When we consider that we are serving the Lord, we realize what a privilege it is to serve because only someone very important could be capable of transmitting God's own power to others.

But this is a capacity that we must acquire, a skill to be learned. Will we let God teach us? Or will we stay fixated on our own petty notions of power and miss out?

December 1

Mary: Hope for the Hopeless

ભ

I ASK YOU NOW TO JOIN IN PRAYING to Mary, that we may place all our concerns and hopes before the heart of Christ. We pray to her in a special way for those who have lost hope and find no reasons to keep fighting, and for those who suffer from injustice, abandonment, and loneliness.

We pray for the elderly, the infirm, children and young people, for all families experiencing difficulty, that Mary may dry their tears, comfort them with a mother's love, and restore their hope and joy.

~Angelus, September 20, 2015

Reflection: When I was in high school, one of my teachers used to pray to St. Jude for us before every class, because St. Jude is the patron of hopeless cases (and, clearly, we were hopeless). Even more than St. Jude, Mary knows what hopelessness looks like: she watched God die on a cross.

Whenever we see someone who has lost hope, or we lose hope ourselves, we can turn to her. She knows everything we're going through: in his dying moments Jesus gave her, as mother, to all of us. She, better than anyone, knows how to comfort us at all times.

December 2

God's Extravagant Love

CR

WE ARE USED TO HEARING that Jesus is the Son of God, that he came out of love to save us, and that he died for us. But we have heard it so many times that we have become accustomed to it....

[When, in fact,] we enter into this mystery of God, of his love, this boundless love, this immense love [we are so] astonished that perhaps we prefer not to understand it: we believe that the style of salvation in which "we do certain things and then we are saved" is better.

Of course, to do good, to do the things that Jesus tells us to do, is good and should be done; [but] the essence of salvation does not come from this [but] comes gratuitously from the love of God.

~Homily, *Domus Sanctae Marthae*,
October 15, 2015

Reflection: Sometimes, when you love someone very much, you decide to get them a really expensive gift. Not because they asked, not because you have to, but because you want to show them what they mean to you. You're not following a rule, you're following your heart: you want your extravagant love to be evident in your extravagant gift.

So many people think of being religious as following the rules. There are rules, but the rules are a byproduct, not the starting point. God came to live and die for us. He could have done it whatever way he wanted, but he chose the gratuitous way of extravagant love.

We do certain things not because they'll save us but to learn to love as our Savior loves: in an extravagant way.

December 3

Following Christ's Great Light

 C℞

"THE PEOPLE WHO WALKED IN DARKNESS have seen a great light" (Is 9:1).

The people who walked—caught up in their activities and routines, amid their successes and failures, their worries and expectations—have seen a great light.

The people who walked—with all their joys and hopes, their disappointments and regrets—have seen a great light....

One special quality of God's people is their ability to see, to contemplate, even in "moments of darkness," the light which Christ brings.

~Homily, Mass, Madison Square Garden,
New York City, September 25, 2015

Reflection: Ever wake up in the middle of the night when you go camping or are out in the country? It can be so very, truly dark—no streetlights, no residual brightness from other houses.

Trying to walk in that darkness is challenging: you're liable to bump into things. Seeing a great light in that darkness—even if it's just a glimpse, just a bit of light that cracks through—makes a huge difference. Because, suddenly, there are shapes in the darkness, a few things that you can be sure of, a way to move forward without fear.

This is what Christ brings: a certainty in our way toward the light.

December 4

God Came into the World Through a Home

ന

HOW IMPORTANT IT IS FOR US to share our home life and to help one another in this marvelous and challenging task of "being a family."…

God did not want to come into the world other than through a family. God did not want to draw near to humanity other than through a home.

~Address, Prayer Vigil, Philadelphia,
September 26, 2015

Reflection: God could have chosen to come to earth any way he wanted. He was God, after all! But he chose the regular way: being born to a human mother, and being part of an everyday human family. He showed us—and still does—that everyday things can still be extraordinary. That our "humble homes" are the place he wants most to be.

Even when we don't feel like being at home, he wants to meet us there.

December 5

Daily Conversion

CR

FOR A CHRISTIAN, CONVERSION IS AN ASSIGNMENT, an everyday task.... One step each day. Every day a step....

Do I want to gossip about someone? Keep quiet, [or]: Am I a bit tired and do not want to pray? Go to pray a little....

Little everyday things [because] the little things ... help us to not give up, to not fall back, to not return to iniquity, but to move forward towards this gift, Jesus' promise that will be the encounter with him.

~Homily, *Domus Sanctae Marthae*, October 22, 2015

Reflection: Sometimes, conversion is hard. Okay, always! There is a little sacrifice, a little mini-death every day. But that sacrifice is what changes things.

When I don't feel ready for a big challenge, I can always say yes to a small one, as long as I keep saying yes. Step by step, the Lord changes us: his grace expands our efforts and spurs us on.

December 6

Life Is Shaped by Our Desire

❦

WHAT IS IT THAT SHAPES YOUR LIFE? What lies deep in your heart? Where do your hopes and aspirations lie? Are you ready to put yourself on the line for the sake of something even greater?

~Address to Students, Havana, Cuba,
September 20, 2015

Reflection: Most kids sit down before Christmas, ready to write their Christmas lists. But many change their lists—sometimes many times—before Christmas.

What do we really want? Do we even know? The more we examine our hearts, the more we realize that what we want is beyond us. Our own deepest desires compel us to put ourselves on the line for something greater; putting ourselves on the line for something greater may even *be* our deepest desire.

December 7

The Greatest Servant

CR

WHO IS THE MOST IMPORTANT? Jesus is straightforward in his reply: "Whoever wishes to be the first—the most important—among you must be the last of all, and the servant of all."

Whoever wishes to be great must serve others, not be served by others.

~Homily, Mass, Havana, Cuba, September 20, 2015

Reflection: We usually think that people with servants are greater or more important than their servants, since the people being served get to make others do their bidding. But if greatness is being like God in all ways, then everything changes.

God came to earth to serve us and lay down his life for us. It is in doing the same that we become great because we become more and more like him. What is greater than that?

December 8
Watch Over Us

ᛒ

MARY, WATCH OVER OUR FAMILIES, our young people, and our elderly. Watch over those who have lost faith and hope. Comfort the sick, the imprisoned, and all who suffer.

~*Regina Caeli*, May 25, 2014

Reflection: Birds watch over their nests to keep predators away and so they can be there when the eggs are ready to hatch. This way, the mother bird can make sure her babies stay safe, get food, and, eventually, learn to fly like she does.

Mary, too, watches over us—she wants to keep evil away from us and help us be fed and grow in goodness and wisdom. Mother Mary, come to us—and as you watch over us, let us watch you, so that we learn to follow your ways.

December 9

Stay Awake

CR

AM I AMONG THOSE WHO, when Jesus asks them to keep watch with him, fall asleep instead, and rather than praying, seek to escape, refusing to face reality?

~Address, Meeting with Priests, Religious, Seminarians,
Mount of Olives, Jerusalem, May 26, 2014

Reflection: It's so easy to be distracted, so easy to ignore unpleasant things or people. We don't answer the phone, or we pretend we didn't hear someone's request, or that we really have to be somewhere else.

It's so easy, we can forget what we're doing. We're avoiding. We're afraid. We don't trust that there is really a light at the end of the tunnel of whatever unpleasant task or person we have to deal with.

Can we learn to trust that our everyday reality is Jesus' way of asking us to keep watch with him?

December 10

Caring for the Vulnerable

CR

THE CALL TO SERVE INVOLVES SOMETHING SPECIAL, to which we must be attentive. Serving means caring for [people's] vulnerability. Caring for the vulnerable of our families, our society, our people.

Theirs are the suffering, fragile, and downcast faces which Jesus tells us specifically to look at and which he asks us to love. With a love which takes shape in our actions and decisions. With a love which finds expression in whatever tasks we ... are called to perform.

~Homily, Mass, Havana, Cuba, September 20, 2015

Reflection: Most of us like receiving gifts, but we much prefer getting presents that someone chose for us personally. We like it when we can tell the gift was chosen with our personal likes and dislikes in mind, and when it's something we really need. When we receive something thoughtful that we need, we realize we are known and loved.

Serving people means serving *specific* people, loving them and giving them what *they* need. True love turns service into the gift of self.

December 11

Building on the Rock of Faith

ର

I INVITE YOU TO BUILD YOUR LIVES on Jesus Christ, on God: the one who builds on God builds on rock, because he is always faithful, even if we sometimes lack faith (cf. 2 Tm 2:13).

~Angelus, September 21, 2014

Reflection: Jesus calls Peter "rock," we learn in the Gospel. The word Jesus used means "pebble" or "small rock." Peter wasn't some massive, immovable rock. He was a rock you could pick up and skip on the water.

But even a pebble comes from rock: it comes from something hard and true and solid; something you can trust not to move. Peter became more and more solid because his faith was in someone greater than himself, because his faith was in the living God.

"Pebble" Peter became the foundation of the Catholic Church. He reminds us that we can all build on the solid rock of Christ. Even when we lack faith (as even Peter sometimes did), we know that in building on Christ we can be certain of our foundation.

December 12

Friends Like Jesus

CR

WE NEED TO BE FRIENDS THE WAY JESUS IS. Not to be closed in on ourselves, but to join his team and play his game, to go out and make more and more friends. To bring the excitement of Jesus' friendship to the world, wherever you find yourselves: at work, at school on WhatsApp, Facebook, or Twitter. When you go out dancing ... or play a little match on the neighborhood field. That is where Jesus' friends can be found.

~Address, Meeting with Young People,
Asunción, Paraguay, July 12, 2015

Reflection: We often think of religion as something we find only in certain places (churches) or certain people (really quiet, pious ones). But we are called to be "in the world," but not "of the world."

What does that mean? It means living, eating, working, playing, doing all the normal things everyone does, which Jesus did, too. But it means that we find our joy in him, not in these things.

When we pursue him and his joy, doing all our regular activities, we find joy in the most unexpected places and people. Looking at the world and knowing he's in it starts to transform everyone and everything, including ourselves.

December 13

Serving People, Not Ideas

 os

CARING FOR OTHERS OUT OF LOVE is not about being servile. Rather, it means putting the question of our brothers and sisters at the center. Service always looks to their faces, touches their flesh, senses their closeness, and even, in some cases, "suffers" that closeness and tries to help them.

Service is never ideological, for we do not serve ideas, we serve people.

~Homily, Mass, Havana, Cuba, September 20, 2015

Reflection: We Christians cannot replace Christ with a program or a set of ideas: Jesus is always concrete, and his coming is always a personal, specific event.

When we serve others in his name, we don't serve "people" in general but individuals whom we are called to love, even when it hurts. That very hurt reminds us that Christ's love is a reality—not an ideology.

December 14

He Chose an Unimportant Place

ର

JESUS WAS BORN IN A FAMILY. He could have come in a spectacular way, or as a warrior, an emperor.... No, no: he is born in a family, in a family ... which he himself formed. He formed it in a remote village on the outskirts of the Roman Empire. Not in Rome, which was the capital of the Empire, not in a big city, but on its nearly invisible outskirts....

And so, right there, on the outskirts of the great empire, began the most holy and good story of Jesus.

~General Audience, December 17, 2014

Reflection: If we think of places we'd like to visit or live, often we think of famous, important places. When it comes to being born, though, we had no choice—we had no say in that! But God *had* a choice—and he chose an unimportant little town, and let his Son be born into a family without power or prestige.

Anytime we think that where we live or what we do is too small to be important to God, let's remember that he chose unimportant people and places for the most important person in the world.

December 15

Changing Hearts

ભ

THE CHRISTIAN JOURNEY is simply about changing hearts. One's own heart first of all, and then helping to transform the hearts of others.... It is about passing from a mentality which domineers, stifles, and manipulates to a mentality which welcomes, accepts, and cares.

~Homily, Mass, Asunción,
Paraguay, July 12, 2015

Reflection: In the story *How the Grinch Stole Christmas*, on the day when the Grinch saw the true joy and lack of selfishness of the Whos down in Whoville, his heart grew three sizes. Seeing people whose happiness really did not depend on material things changed him permanently.

This is just the tip of the iceberg! Seeing people who love and give in the face of suffering and pain transforms everything. Christ wants to make a new heart within me.

December 16

Whom We Adore

CR

WE ARE *A PEOPLE WHO ADORE* GOD. We adore God who is love, who in Jesus Christ gave himself for us, offered himself on the cross ... and by the power of this love rose from the dead and lives in his Church....

We Christians don't want to worship anything and anyone in this world except for Jesus Christ, who is present in the Holy Eucharist.

~Homily, Mass, Calabria, Italy, June 21, 2015

Reflection: When we call someone or something adorable, usually we mean that it's really, really cute. It's sort of funny that a word so closely related to God should also mean cute, but it reminds us, too, of the tender affection God has for us. He wanted to make himself known and loved in a way we humans could understand. So he even became a baby: someone easy to love—adorable!

Baby Jesus grew up and eventually died for us, but the whole path of his life was a way of leading us from our natural affection for a little child all the way to a grown-up love that includes suffering and death: adorable in the full and deep sense of the word.

Jesus shows us that adoring God doesn't leave anything out of life.

December 17

Willing to Listen to God's Call

CR

WHEN LIFE PROVES DIFFICULT AND DEMANDING, we can be tempted to step back, turn away and withdraw ... and thus flee the responsibility of doing our part as best we can.

Do you remember what happened to Elijah? From a human point of view, the prophet was afraid and tried to run away. Afraid. "Elijah was afraid; he got up and fled for his life.... He walked for forty days and forty nights to Horeb, the mountain of God. At that place he came to a cave and spent the night there. Then the word of the Lord came to him, saying: 'What are you doing here, Elijah?'" (1 Kgs 19:3,8-9).

On Horeb, he would get his answer not in the great wind which shatters the rocks, not in the earthquake, nor even in the fire.

God's grace does not shout out; it is a whisper which reaches all those who are ready to hear the gentle breeze—that still, small voice. It urges them to go forth, to return to the world, to be witnesses to God's love for mankind, so that the world may believe.

~Homily, Vigil in Preparation for the
Synod of Bishops, Rome, October 3, 2015

Reflection: Sometimes, we wish God would make what we're supposed to do more obvious. "If he would just show me more clearly," we think.

But many people who have had the most direct contact with God wanted to ignore him some of the time—like Elijah! Sometimes, we just don't want to do what he asks of us. Which is why he speaks to us with a small voice—that way he can tell if we are willing to listen. If not, we won't hear him.

But, just like a mother who tries lovingly to wake her child, he keeps repeating himself.

December 18

The Problem with Conspicuous Consumption

ભ

TODAY, CONSUMPTION SEEMS TO DETERMINE what is important. Consuming relationships, consuming friendships … consuming, consuming. Whatever the cost or consequences. A consumption which does not favor bonding, a consumption which has little to do with human relationships….

The important thing is no longer our neighbor, with his or her familiar face, story, and personality.

~Address, Meeting with Bishops,
Philadelphia, September 27, 2015

Reflection: Sometimes, we might think it's better to avoid really committing ourselves to people. We let ourselves cycle through relationships for what they can give us and then we move on.

This is called using people—consuming them and tossing them aside. We treat them like objects that can do something for us here and there: give us a ride someplace, provide some entertainment, or maybe even get us a job.

When we use others, we never get to know them as people, and we don't allow God to work in the relationship as he intends. Am I guilty of using others? If so, how can the Lord help me to recognize and correct that tendency?

December 19

Faith Is Not for the Fainthearted

CR

FAITH IS NO REFUGE FOR THE FAINTHEARTED, but something which enhances our lives. It makes us aware of a magnificent calling, the vocation of love ... for it is based on God's faithfulness which is stronger than our every weakness.

~*Lumen Fidei*, June 29, 2013

Reflection: A friend's mother once said that when she got married she thought it would be like a boat coming into harbor, but instead she found she was setting out to sea.

Faith is like this: it is not a refuge, but a call to something greater and more beautiful. Even the fainthearted don't need to be afraid, because God's faithfulness and strength are greater than we can imagine.

December 20

In God's Hands

ca

[MARY] TEACHES US TO PUT OUR FAMILIES in God's hands; she teaches us to pray, to kindle the hope which shows us that our concerns are also God's concerns.

> ~Homily, Mass for Families,
> Guayaquil, Ecuador, July 6, 2015

Reflection: We might think that Mary always knew that she had God on her side, being Jesus' mother and all. And she did—but it's not because challenging things didn't happen to her! Think how hard it must have been in Bethlehem, wanting to have her baby someplace. And she got a manger. It wasn't what she was looking for, but it had what she needed. God cares about our problems, even if his answers may look strange.

Mary, teach me to pray as you did, and to trust!

December 21

Who Are We?

CR

WHO ARE WE, AS WE STAND BEFORE THE CHILD JESUS? Who are we, as we stand before today's children? Are we like Mary and Joseph, who welcomed Jesus and cared for him with the love of a father and a mother? Or are we like Herod, who wanted to eliminate him?

Are we like the shepherds, who went in haste to kneel before him in worship and offer him their humble gifts? Or are we indifferent?...

Are we ready to be there for children, to "waste time" with them? Are we ready to listen to them, to care for them, to pray for them and with them? Or do we ignore them because we are too caught up in our own affairs?

~Homily, Mass, Bethlehem, Pilgrimage
to the Holy Land, May 25, 2014

Reflection: Most of us feel like we know ourselves better than anyone else. But then, sometimes, something happens, or we meet someone and it changes our ideas about who we are.

This happened when Jesus was born. His birth changed the history of the world: he unsettled the whole world. That challenged many people in power and demands our attention today just as it did for the Magi and the shepherds.

These men—learned and foreign, humble and simple—didn't come to help out with the baby; they didn't come to fulfill any social obligations. They came in wonder.

Who am I, as I contemplate the Christ Child? If I find myself impatient or violent in front of his presence, can I rediscover the wonder he came to ignite in me? Can I let go of my own concerns and learn to adore him?

December 22

The Lamplight of Faith

☙

FAITH IS NOT A LIGHT WHICH SCATTERS ALL OUR DARKNESS, but a lamp which guides our steps in the night.

~*Lumen Fidei*, June 29, 2013

Reflection: Some people like to make long-term life plans—what they'll be doing in five years, where they'll retire, what kind of wedding dress they'll wear, etc. Some people like to plan ahead. But life isn't always so cooperative with our plans, and we can sometimes feel like we're plodding ahead in the dark. The light of faith is a great help to us, because it helps us see what's ahead and what step we must take next. But we're impatient and often wonder why God can't let us see farther up the road.

We need to remember that God doesn't want to be our map—he wants to come with us. Our steps may seem slow, but we have someone else on the road with us, which is much better than any road atlas or GPS.

December 23

No Place in the Inn

Ɑ

[St.] Joseph had to face some difficult situations in his life. One of them was the time when Mary was about to give birth, to have Jesus. The Bible tells us that "while they were [in Bethlehem], the time came for her to deliver her child. And she gave birth to her firstborn son and wrapped him in bands of cloth, and laid him in a manger, because there was no place for them in the inn" (Lk 2:6-7).

The Bible is very clear about this: there was no room for them. I can imagine Joseph, with his wife about to have a child, with no shelter, no home, no place to stay.

The Son of God came into this world as a homeless person. The Son of God knew what it was to start life without a roof over his head. We can imagine what poor Joseph must have been thinking: what a way to start life as a family!

~Address, Charitable Center, St. Patrick Parish,
Washington, D.C., September 24, 2015

Reflection: Have you ever felt like you were the one who let down your team? Like you messed up and people you care about are paying the price? It would have been easy for St. Joseph to feel that way, looking for a place for Mary to have baby Jesus and not being able to find anything.

He wasn't the baby's biological father, but he was a father to him in every other way. Joseph was responsible for Jesus, and he loved both his wife and his son; even if he didn't feel guilty, he must have felt sad that there was no better place for God's son.

But this was the way God wanted to be born, not because St. Joseph failed, but because God wanted to start life in the humblest way. He doesn't want us to forget that. When we feel humiliated, let us think of Joseph and ask for his intercession, that we may find the Lord instead of feelings of failure.

December 24

The Name God Wants Is Emmanuel

ભ

GOD DID NOT WANT ANY OTHER NAME FOR HIMSELF than Emmanuel (cf. Mt 1:23). He is "God with us." This was his desire from the beginning, his purpose, his constant effort to say to us: "I am God with you, I am God for you."

~Address, Prayer Vigil, Philadelphia,
September 26, 2015

Reflection: God chose to reveal himself to a people who had a very clear idea of God. For the ancient Israelites, God wasn't an everyday character with great powers and everyday human weaknesses as the gods were for some other cultures. God in the Jewish tradition was someone whose name you couldn't even say out loud, that's how great he was.

And it was *that* God who chose to be *with* us. *The* God: the one who knows everything and can do everything. He's above us, showing us the way, but he's also here. Right here, right now. There is no one greater, and there is no greater gift.

December 25

A Family with Open Doors

GOD CAME INTO THE WORLD IN A FAMILY. And he could do this because that family was a family with a heart open to love, a family whose doors were open. We can think of Mary, a young woman. She couldn't believe it: "How can this be?" But once it was explained to her, she obeyed.

We think of Joseph, full of dreams for making a home; then along comes this surprise which he doesn't understand. He accepts; he obeys.

And in the loving obedience of this woman, Mary, and this man, Joseph, we have a family into which God comes.

~Address, Prayer Vigil, Philadelphia,
September 26, 2015

Reflection: Most people these days keep their front door locked. But if they're having a party, they will often unlock it so that it's easier for friends to come in, even if they still plan to answer the door. When a door is locked, it takes time to unlock it.

The same is true of our hearts as well. If we get used to keeping them locked, it takes more time to open them, which means that love moves more slowly. We lock our hearts for the same reason we lock our doors—we're afraid of bad people getting in.

But God wants us to open our hearts to him. He asks us to welcome the stranger, the difficult neighbor, the new child, the handicapped child, someone else's child ... the presence of a person we didn't expect. They are his way of bringing his mysterious new life into the world, just as in Nazareth more than 2,000 years ago.

December 26

He Makes His Kingdom Grow

ભ

[THE] WORD [OF GOD], IF ACCEPTED, CERTAINLY BEARS FRUIT, for God himself makes it sprout and grow in ways that we cannot always … understand (cf. Mt 4:27).

All this tells us that it is always God, it is always God who makes his kingdom grow. That is why we fervently pray, "thy kingdom come." It is he who makes it grow.

~Angelus, June 14, 2015

Reflection: At the end of many fairy tales, the good characters get to be king and queen and live happily ever after: the kingdom—the world—is theirs!

The kingdom of God is a more mysterious thing: God reigns and yet he is not in charge the way a typical king and queen are, making all the decisions. For example, he leaves much of this to us. But he does make his kingdom grow, if we are patient, faithful, and keep a lookout.

For he wants for us to live happily ever after with him, in this world and the next.

December 27

The Same Christ

THE CHRIST, WHO [COMES TO US IN THE EUCHARIST] is the same One who comes to us in the everyday happenings; he is in the poor person who holds out his hand, in the suffering one who begs for help, in the brother or sister who asks for our availability and awaits our welcome. He is in the child who knows nothing about Jesus or salvation, who does not have faith. He is in every human being, even the smallest and the defenseless.

~Angelus, June 7, 2015

Reflection: The sacramental mystery of the Eucharist—that bread and wine are changed into the body and blood of Christ, while still looking and seeming like ordinary bread and wine—is difficult to understand.

But it's true: Christ wanted to give himself so completely to us that he wanted us to be able to even eat and digest him, for us to know where to find him and be able to receive him.

When I go into a Catholic church or chapel, that awareness changes my way of being present in that space. It's equally mysterious how Christ can be present in everyday circumstances and people. And yet, he is. That is how much he wants to be with us, that he finds a way in all kinds of places, peoples, and circumstances.

December 28

Trust Him

☙

TRUST CHRIST, LISTEN TO HIM, follow in his footsteps. He never abandons us, not even in the darkest moments of our lives. He is our hope.

~Greeting to Sick Children, July 24, 2014

Reflection: Sometimes, when we are sick, doctors tell us to do things we don't understand. But if our doctors are good, we trust them and follow their recommendations even if we don't quite get it.

Jesus is the best doctor we have, because he knows how to cure our soul-sickness, the darkness that's in our heart. We can always trust him to do what's best for us, even when we don't like the medicine he gives us.

Jesus, help me to trust and hope in you!

December 29
A Soft Knock

ↁ

[THE] CALLING OF THE LORD is expressed with such humility and respect in the text from the Book of Revelation: "Look, I am at the door and I am calling; do you want to open the door?" (cf. 3:20). He does not use force, he does not break the lock, but instead, quite simply, he presses the doorbell, knocks gently on the door, and then waits. This is our God!

~Homily, Mass, Quito, Bolivia, July 7, 2015

Reflection: People often complain when someone enters their room (or their house) without knocking. They feel disrespected. But if they're not paying attention, or they're playing loud music, they can't hear someone knock.

If we're expecting someone, we keep on the lookout and try not to be too loud. God is always respectful with us; he is humble and gentle, but sometimes we complain about it! Sometimes, we wish that God were easier to find, that he were more obvious in our lives. He knocks, but we have to be listening and paying attention. His gentle love is worth looking out for.

December 30

Looking Back in Order to Move Forward

☙

TO KEEP MOVING FORWARD IN LIFE, in addition to knowing where we want to go, we also need to know who we are and where we come from. Individuals or peoples who have no memory and erase their past risk losing their identity and destroying their future.

So we need to remember who we are, and in what our spiritual and moral heritage consists.

~Address to Students, Havana, Cuba,
September 20, 2015

Reflection: When we are getting along well with someone, we often remember good moments we've spent with them, but when they upset us, we dwell on less happy memories.

How we treat others and interact with them may depend on what we remember. Memory seems like something that's "just there," but we also get to choose how we use it. We have a past, but if we ignore it, or ignore important parts of it, we risk losing the parts of our lives that are most important.

December 31

Faith Makes Us Neighbors

CR

I WOULD LIKE [TO] THINK FOR A MOMENT about Joseph and Mary in Bethlehem. They were forced to leave home, families, and friends. They had to leave all that they had ... to go somewhere else, to a place where they knew no one, a place where they had no house, no family.

That was when that young couple had Jesus. That was how, having made preparations as best they could in a cave, they gave us Jesus. They were alone, in a strange land, just the three of them. Then, all of a sudden, people began to appear: shepherds, people just like them who had to leave their homes to find better opportunities for their families....

When they heard that Jesus had been born, they went to see him. They became neighbors. In an instant, they became a family to Mary and Joseph. The family of Jesus.

This is what happens when Jesus comes into our lives. It is what happens with faith. Faith brings us closer. It makes us neighbors. It makes us neighbors to others.

~Address, Visit to the People of Bañado Norte,
Asunción, Paraguay, July 12, 2015

Reflection: Why did the shepherds and others draw near to Jesus? Because they had heard there was something amazing to see—something spectacular and worth their time. It was "just a baby in a manger"—but not *just* a baby in a manger!

Something similar happens for us. When people encounter Jesus and are changed by him, we are drawn to them. We sense the opportunity to witness something amazing. Jesus wants to come to us through everyday circumstances and "ordinary" people—who in him are anything but ordinary.

But it's up to us to draw near—to them and to him.

About the Editor

❦

REBECCA VITZ CHERICO is the oldest of six children and grew up in an apartment in New York City. She received her BA in Italian from Yale College and her PhD in Spanish literature from New York University. She is currently a part-time instructor of Spanish at Villanova University. Rebecca and her husband, Colin, live in the greater Philadelphia area and have five children.